THE
SOUTH DOWNS
NATIONAL PARK

Chanctonbury Ring (© airscapes.co.uk)

THE
SOUTH DOWNS
NATIONAL PARK

ARCHAEOLOGICAL
WALKING GUIDES

JOHN MANLEY

First published 2013

The History Press
The Mill, Brimscombe Port
Stroud, Gloucestershire, GL5 2QG
www.thehistorypress.co.uk

British Library Cataloguing in Publication Data.
A catalogue record for this book is available from the British Library.

ISBN 978 0 7524 6608 8

Typesetting and origination by The History Press
Printed in Great Britain

CONTENTS

Acknowledgements 7
Author's Note on Periods and Dates 8
Preamble to Walking in the Park 9
The Archaeology of the Park: Themes While You Walk 13

The Walks 65

1 February: Stanmer Park and Hollingbury Hill Fort –
the Edge of Brighton 65

2 March: Lewes Town –
In the Footsteps of William and Gundrada 74

3 March: Down to Jevington and Back 83

4 April: Devil's Dyke, Saddlescombe and Wolstonbury Hill 91

5 April: Truleigh Hill, Edburton Castle and Thundersbarrow 98

6 April: Harrow Hill and Britain's First Miners 106

7 May: Chanctonbury Ring and the Ring-Planter 114

8 May: Stane Street Steps 121

9 May: Trotton and Iping Common – From Heath to River 129

10 June: Harting Down to … West Virginia 137

11 June: Black Down – The Temple of the Winds 145

12 June: Petersfield – The Town by the Lake 153

13 June: Up and Down Old Winchester Hill 161

14 July: Selborne – On the Trail of Gilbert White,
Famous Antiquarian 169

15 July: St Catherine's Hill, Winchester – There be Dragons … 178

Getting Around the Park 187

General References 189

Index 191

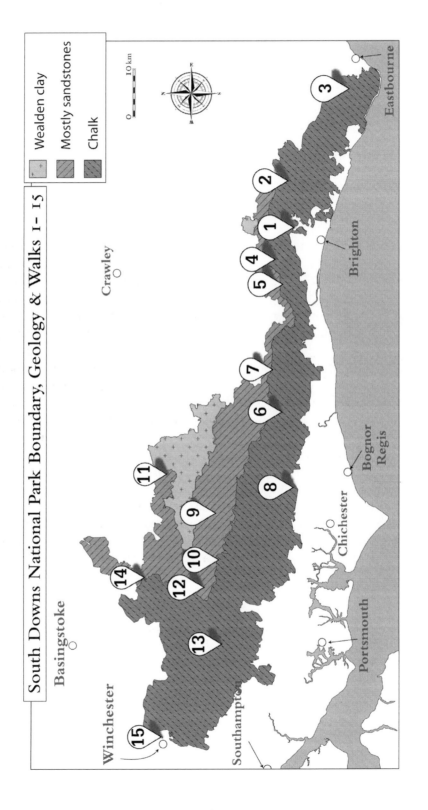

South Downs National Park Boundary, Geology & Walks 1– 15

ACKNOWLEDGEMENTS

This work is based on the efforts of generations of historians and archae-ologists who have studied the past of the area now designated as the South Downs National Park. Their enquiries have made these pages possible. In par-ticular I am in the debt of several people who commented on an earlier draft of parts of the text: Professors Peter Drewett, Brian Short and Robin Milner-Gulland (University of Sussex), Dr Mark Gardiner (Queen's University, Belfast), David Hopkins (Hampshire County Archaeologist), David McOmish (English Heritage), David Allen (Hampshire Museum Service), James Kenny (Chichester District Archaeologist), and Casper Johnson and Greg Shuter (East Sussex County Council Archaeologists). Particular comments on specific walks were gratefully received from John Funnell (Brighton & Hove Archaeological Society), John Bleach (Sussex Archaeological Society), David Thompson, Heather Warne, Janet Pennington, David Bone, Colin Mattingly (Petersfield Area Historical Society), Greta Turner (Haslemere Museum), Michael Shapland (Jevington), David Baker and Edward Yates (on Selborne), and David Elliott (National Trust). Their col-lective critique filled in the many holes in my understanding and steadied my grammar. The illustrations are my own, unless otherwise acknowledged. I am in debt to Russell Oliver for his dramatic aerial images. Thanks also to Dora Kemp and Natural England for permission to reproduce their maps in the colour section. My greatest gratitude I reserve for my partner, Lesley. She accompanied me on all these walks, often pointing out things I had not seen, listening to sounds beyond my hearing range, spotting camera angles I was blind to, sensing feelings I would not have felt, as well as packing lunches I could not have packed. We walked quite a bit, and talked quite a bit more. Hence this book.

John Manley,
Autumn 2012

AUTHOR'S NOTE ON PERIODS AND DATES

Please note that dates in this work are expressed with reference to the Common Era, either Before Common Era (BCE) or Common Era (CE). Thus 1805 CE corresponds to AD 1805, and 700 BCE corresponds to 700 BC. A 'c.' in front of a date stands for *circa*, meaning approximately.

Expressions such as sixteenth century or eighteenth century usually refer to the Common Era, unless otherwise indicated; so sixteenth century refers to the years 1501–1600 CE, and eighteenth century equates with the years 1701–1800 CE, and so on. In the twentieth century the dates for the First World War are 1914–18 and for the Second World War they are 1939–45.

Conventional archaeological and historic period labels are used sparingly in the text. For the sake of clarification, the principal ones, relevant to the South Downs National Park, are provided here:

Period	Approximate Date Range
Palaeolithic (Old Stone Age)	450,000 BCE to 9000 BCE
Mesolithic (Middle Stone Age)	9000 BCE to 4000 BCE
Neolithic (New Stone Age)	4000 BCE to 2500 BCE
Bronze Age	2500 BCE to 700 BCE
Iron Age	700 BCE to 43 CE
Roman	43 CE to 410 CE
Saxon	410 CE to 1066 CE
Medieval	1066 CE to 1500 CE
Early Modern	1500 CE to 1750 CE
Modern	1750 CE onwards

PREAMBLE TO WALKING IN THE PARK

The South Downs National Park extends from the outskirts of Eastbourne, in East Sussex, to the edge of Winchester, in Hampshire. It consists of a considerable chunk of southern England and contains an extraordinary variety of archaeological and historic monuments. You can explore the camps, flint mines and tombs of the earliest farmers, walk around great earthen banks bounding Iron Age hill forts, stroll along Roman roads, visit Saxon churches, medieval castles and houses, and examine the remains of industry and more recent military conflicts. Take a walk anywhere in the Park and you will find yourself wandering into the past; after all, most modern footpaths follow very old tracks. There is such lot to see, and the good news is that all of it is free to access.

But how do you start? That's where this book comes in. Here are fifteen walks back in time throughout the length and breadth of the Park. They are described in the order my partner and I walked them, starting off near Brighton, going first east towards Eastbourne and then travelling westwards all the way to Winchester. We walked them intermittently, starting in February 2012 and finishing by July. We became so used to planning and exploring these walks that we felt a little lost when the last one was completed. Most of our journeys are rural, but there are two urban walks: Lewes and Petersfield. So, if you want to explore the past of the Park but don't know which area to pick first or what route to take, read on and join us.

Before introducing the archaeology of the Park, however, we would like to say a little bit about walking, or rather *recreational* walking. People in remote prehistory obviously walked everywhere, but probably for particular purposes – to go down to the river to fish or the forest to hunt or the fields to look after the cattle. But even in prehistory some walking was ceremonial – to bury the dead or to go on a pilgrimage to a place of worship. There may have been ritual processions, for instance along the 'Avenue' that leads to Stonehenge. Much later, the Roman philosopher Seneca, advisor to Emperor Nero, wrote about escaping from the city and the odour of the kitchens to enjoy the healthy countryside, especially his vineyards. Carefully enclosed medieval pleasure gardens were places of religious symbolism for the elite as well as centres of sensory and earthly delights. Recreational walking for the masses, in the sense of appreciation of landscapes

The South Downs Way near Bignor Hill, looking east. The dip slope of the Downs slopes gradually downwards from the north scarp (left to right).

and enjoyment of wild, open spaces, began in Britain in the early nineteenth century, when workers wanted to escape the polluted cityscapes spawned by the Industrial Revolution.

Britain has come to have a great recreational walking tradition, therefore, and a great tradition of walking writers. In the nineteenth century George Borrow spent forty years exploring England, Wales and Europe on foot. His book, *Wild Wales*, was published in 1857 and recorded long walks throughout Wales made in the second half of 1854. Edward Thomas, soldier, poet and author, wrote books on the Icknield Way (a possible prehistoric track from the Chilterns to the Brecklands of East Anglia) and the south country at the start of the twentieth century. Alfred Wainwright wrote his first love letter to the fells of the Lake District in 1955. More recently the walking genre has been documented by such gifted writers as Christopher Somerville and Robert Macfarlane. Walking has become a well-organised leisure pursuit, with thousands of footpaths and long-distance trails, and countless websites and magazines devoted to walking. Outdoor shops are full of walking equipment and, of course, the Ramblers Association exists to promote this fulfilling pastime.

The South Downs National Park, with its celebrated South Downs Way, is an integral piece of this walking industry. And walking is clearly good for you. It keeps you fit and gets you off those sofas and into the fresh air. In the context of an archaeological walking guide, by means of walking you experience most of the monuments of the past in the same way as the people who built, lived and frequented them – through your body and on your feet. We are grateful to Tim Ingold for reminding us that much modern travel (by car, bus or plane) involves enforced immobility and sensory deprivation. It breaks the intimate bond between movement and bodily perception. So the practice of walking, especially in a rural environment, has a reconnecting effect. It's a simple thing to observe but walkers in the South Downs National Park usually greet each other with a 'morning' or 'afternoon' or just 'hi' given quickly *en passant*. Does this arise from recognition of a shared leisure activity or from the walking-in-the-countryside act itself?

Some of those famous writers saw other beneficial effects. Some took to walking to try to overcome more serious concerns: a melancholia that could not be shaken off by other means. This is walking as an anti-depressant. We also have an inkling that the French eighteenth-century philosopher Rousseau knew about some of the less obvious, more cerebral, benefits of walking. Towards the end of his life, in the fourth book of his *Confessions*, he wrote: 'I can only meditate when I am walking … when I stop I cease to think; my mind only works with my legs.' For a philosopher this is remarkably straightforward. We do think that there is a certain kind of thinking, and a particular sort of conversation, that can only be had while walking.

But let's get more grounded: our fifteen walks in the South Downs National Park are themed around archaeology and history. None of the walks are particularly long. They can all be taken in the space of a few hours. You don't need to start out at dawn, and you will get home before dusk. Most of our walks are divided up into morning and afternoon halves, not least to give us time to find a place to enjoy a packed lunch. Walking times are quoted for each of the walks but you should double these at least to give yourself time for the 'standing and staring' and simply strolling around an earthwork or building. We recommend that you then add in about forty-five minutes for lunch.

Most of all these walks are about trying to immerse yourself in the layered history of the Park's past. These are not route marches; they are not about trying to get from A to B. It is just a little sad when you see people bent on getting to X or Y by dusk in the South Downs National Park, walking, sometimes running, over the subtle humps and bumps that could tell them a lot more if only they would stop to look. It feels like a missed opportunity. To paraphrase Ingold again: we want to enjoy the trails and paths that link our monuments, as much as the monuments themselves. We walk with time, not against it.

We have also not sought out challenging climbs or tricky descents. The landscape is there to be respected and thought about. It is not throwing down a gauntlet. And most of the walks are circular, returning you to your point of departure. We are amateur walkers undertaking archaeological ambles at a pace considerably slower than leisurely.

Before we set out it is as well to lay out for you an introduction to the South Downs National Park, its archaeology and history. If you read this before trying out one of our walks, a lot more of what you see will fit into a broader context. And one last thing: even if you never intend to take one of these walks, or if you live far from the South Downs such that you visiting them is unlikely, impossible even, then we hope you can still discover something in this book to fire your imagination. We tried to write up these walks in a way that sometimes blends the past with the present. The walks are frequently populated with people from the past, with their monuments, buildings and burial mounds, and, of course, ourselves. Like Richard Jefferies in Gloucestershire in 1887, approaching a Bronze Age barrow on a gloriously hot day, feeling as if he could 'look back and feel *then*; the sunshine of *then*, and their life', we try to conjure up that sensation, tell stories, bring something of the sunshine of past lives on the South Downs to you, wherever you are.

THE ARCHAEOLOGY OF THE PARK: THEMES WHILE YOU WALK

ON TOP OF THE WORLD

For those of you who have already visited the undulating hills of the South Downs, you will know that, whatever your mood, it is hard not to feel exhilarated by the experience of standing on the edge of its precipitous north scarp, gazing out over the gently ribbed expanse of the wooded Weald. The naturalist William Henry Hudson wrote: 'during the whole fifty-three mile length from Beachy Head to Harting the ground never rises above a height of 850 feet, but we feel on top of the world.' And it's true – we do. With shape-shifting fluffy clouds drifting across a blue sky, and the sun resting between your shoulders, you can really feel 'on top of the world'. But give yourself an additional treat. Walk along a little and turn through 180 degrees. Just occasionally, across the stretches of downland to the south, you glimpse along a dry valley and a flat flash of blue appears on the horizon – the sun winks back at you from the English Channel. People have lived and visited the Downs for thousands of years. Did they have similar feelings when admiring these views, or not? Did they think the Downs were 'special'? There are some clues, and they lie in the traces they left behind. We want to walk with you and discover them.

People have lived, hunted, farmed, worshipped, gathered together and buried their dead in the area now designated the South Downs National Park for over 8,000 years, and they continue to do so. Long before that time, human activity in the Park was intermittent, largely dependent on whether the cold episodes of the last Ice Age permitted occupation at all. The earliest human activity was discovered at Boxgrove, just on the southern boundary of the Park, north-east of Chichester (Walk 8). There, beautifully fashioned flint tools and animal bones indicate the presence of several families of hunters in the very remote past; it's difficult to imagine, but they were there around 400,000 years ago. Much more recently, by some 8,000 years ago, the climate had warmed up considerably and bands of people who lived by hunting, gathering and fishing came to the Downs and stayed. Human beings have been there ever since.

Despite its name, the South Downs National Park is not simply the chalk Downs, although these rounded hills, running in a continuous line from east to west, do

A sandy pathway across the heather on Stedham Common (Walk 9).

Woods that cloak the hillsides – called 'hangers' – are particularly a feature of the western end of the South Downs National Park.

constitute a sort of geological vertebrae. At the much larger western end, the Park extends considerably to the north to include the valley of the Rother with its lowland heaths, and then beyond to the sandstones and greensands that are much more dominant than in the east and give rise to a distinctive feel for the landscape and vegetation. With hill slopes supporting oak, hazel, ash, beech and elm, these sandstone ridges are famous for their 'hangers' – dense cloaks of tree cover that cling tenaciously to their sides. Indeed, the highest point in the South Downs National Park is not on the Downs, but at Black Down (280m), south of Haslemere, where the sandstone supports dense stands of pine and a cover of heather (Walk 11).

The different groups of people in the area now included in the Park, over this very long period of time, have both exploited its natural resources and often left behind a legacy of their presence. They have quarried the chalk and mined the flint, hunted its animals, fished its bisecting rivers and collected its wild plants, berries, nuts and fungi. They have coppiced its woods, ploughed its fields and lined dew ponds with clay to catch its rainfall. They used some of the resources – earth, timber, chalk, greensand, sandstone and flint – to build structures and craft objects to make their lives more comfortable and more meaningful. At various times they constructed houses to live in, of all shapes and sizes, from round to rectangular, from simple to grand. They sank fish traps, pioneered trackways and roads, and constructed earthen banks around deer parks; laid out ditches and hedges to surround fields, put up sheep pens, built mills to catch downland winds and turn grain into flour, and built brick waterworks, like those at Twyford, to supply water. In times of crisis great complexes of ditches and banks could be erected, or towering stone citadels to dominate and repel, and more recently brick and concrete installations to guard and defend threats from the air and sea.

But then, as now, life was not just about practicalities of existence. People built special places where they could meet in larger gatherings than usual, swapping stories, continuing old rivalries or finding partners. Places where they could joke, feast, gamble, compete and generally enjoy themselves. To appease, enlist the support of or worship ancestral figures or singular deities people resorted to a variety of activities which have left their mark, especially on the Downs. They gathered together to sacrifice objects and bury them in the ground; they erected temples to all manner of gods; closer to our era they fashioned great places of communal worship – churches, chapels, monasteries and priories; some people today venerate a chalk figure at Wilmington. Lastly, the Park area has been the final resting place for many. The thousands of prehistoric round earthen mounds or 'barrows', which must have once formed necklace-like lines along the imposing north scarp of the Downs, attest to places of mourning and memory, as do the tombstones of lower-lying medieval churchyards. Today the tradition continues: the Chattri Monument north of Brighton commemorates the cremations of Sikh and Hindu soldiers who fought for the British. Clayton Wood, south of Hassocks, provides a green alternative to traditional cemeteries, offering services for scattering of ashes and eco-friendly burials within sight of Jack and Jill windmills.

Very few regions on earth have all the resources that human beings, with their capacity for invention and imagination, require. Rich in chalk, flint and woodland, and with some well-drained, fertile soils, the Park region has few clay sources to exploit, relatively little workable stone for building and no metal sources. Some of these things, therefore, had to be brought from both near and far: for building, greensand (predominantly at the western end of the Park) or quality limestone from Caen in Normandy; clay for ceramics and bricks came from places such as Burgess Hill, just to the north of the Park, while iron-rich deposits were plentiful in the Weald. Museums, in and around the Park, are full of things that gave comfort and ultimately meaning to lives in the past: flint tools, ceramic cooking pots, bronze spearheads, iron fire backs, wooden furniture, all manner of textiles and clothing, tokens, jewellery and even golden rings declaring everlasting love. But not everything has found its way into museums. Even today, walking on broken downland ground, you may be lucky enough to spot a 4,000-year-old flint scraper that was once used to prepare an animal hide for a garment, its serrated edge still sharp, still serviceable.

The South Downs National Park therefore contains a long legacy of earthworks, buildings and objects left by previous generations, and each successive generation was faced by the challenge of what to do with the things it had inherited. Sometimes they simply neglected them, reused them or deliberately destroyed them, but often they were more circumspect. For instance, the people who dug the great ditch around Old Winchester Hill in the Iron Age drove their perimeter ditch through much earlier Bronze Age barrows (Walk 13). Almost certainly they knew these mounds were burial places of people long ago and, probably for that reason, inside their hill fort they left intact another three very prominent barrows – it was a question of respect and veneration, perhaps even compensation for the dead they had disturbed. In like manner, occasional finds of prehistoric objects by occupants of the region during the Roman period were treated with curiosity and kept for reverential reasons, or just simply as good-luck charms. The reuse of Roman bricks in Saxon churches suggests a more prosaic connection. And spare a thought, as your train speeds up out of Lewes station, Brighton bound, for the founders of Lewes Priory, William de Warenne and his wife Gundrada. Their bodies were disturbed during the building of the line in 1845 and their remains laid to rest (again) in the nearby church of St John the Baptist, in Southover (Walk 2).

In this short introduction to the archaeology of the South Downs National Park we want to pick out, highly selectively, some of the special places and sites left behind by past communities who have lived, hunted, farmed, worked or simply occasionally visited the region. It will also become obvious to you that our 'archaeology' encompasses not only material remains from the remote past but also from the quite recent. To emphasise this theme we want to stress that there are some threads (as well as some ruptures) linking those families 6,000 years ago, who may have gathered at Whitehawk, above Brighton or the Trundle, near Chichester, and ourselves. We will point out easily accessible monuments which you can visit, and tell you about some sites where traces of the past are hidden or have disappeared, and where your imagination will have to do the work. When you do so you can reflect on how the experience of being in the Park (admittedly an artificial construct that has little historical validity) once shaped past lives and now shapes yours. To that end, rather than set out the content of this introduction in chronological or geographical sections, we have opted to let each brief section tell the story of some enduring activities that transcend generational fault lines. To relate a more meaningful and complete narrative of the past we occasionally wander outside the Park boundaries. But first we begin with stories from the earth itself.

FROM THE EARTH

Much of the rock beneath the resiliently springy turf of the South Downs consists of bands of white or greyish chalk, and nodules or horizontal slabs of black or grey flint. The chalk (which is a very pure form of limestone, up to 95 per cent calcium carbonate) was deposited in extraordinarily different conditions from those we live in today. A warm, shallow tropical sea covered most of north-west Europe between 65 and 100 million years ago. Chalk was formed by billions of slowly sinking microscopic plankton, known as *coccoliths*, whose minute skeletons gradually amassed on the sea floor; the tiny white bones gave the rock its distinctive colour. However, the tectonic plates of Africa and Europe were inching closer together. Their eventual collision pushed up the Himalayas, the Alps and raised a chalk dome covering what we now call south-east England. Subsequent erosion weathered away the soft top of the dome, leaving the North and South Downs facing each other across the older clays of the Weald. The South Downs were gradually sculpted into discrete chalk blocks as river valleys were carved out by the Cuckmere, Ouse, Adur and Arun. In Hampshire, too, higher areas of chalk were isolated by the rivers Meon and Itchen. The combination of freeze-thaw erosion cycles during the relatively recent Ice Ages weathered out some of the Downs' characteristic dry valleys, such as the celebrated Devil's Dyke, north of Brighton (Walk 4).

So much for the geological history. The real importance of the chalk Downs to early generations lay in its more obviously apparent features. The oldest chalk lies under the higher elevations of the north scarp, and from there it is possible to see across the Weald of south-east England to the greensand hills of Surrey and the chalk of the North Downs. The lower rises and falls of the sands and clays of the Weald thus seem framed and encircled by a greensand and downland ring. It can be no coincidence that many of the major prehistoric monuments in the South Downs National Park were sited to make use of such sweeping views, and for the same reason the South Downs Way tracks the north scarp for much of its length. Underfoot, when wet, chalk paths turn to a cloying greyish mulch, but in the droughts of summer the chalk crumbles so that driven cattle can kick up clouds

Looking from the river Itchen at Winchester across towards the Hospital of St Cross (Walk 15).

of white dust behind them. It was this whiteness of the chalk that was also attractive to builders of earthworks. Those earthen banks around the many Iron Age hill forts and the countless prehistoric burial mounds, now so deceptively grass-covered and blending into green backdrops all too easily, were once gleaming and white, beacons of light that shone out and defiantly marked their presence.

For much of the prehistoric period, the black gold of the Downs lay in the tabular seams of flint layered within the chalk (Walk 6). Flint, ultimately derived from plankton, was laid in bands or nodules of silica in the chalk. Before the advent of metals, flint could be worked into all manner of tools for cutting, scraping, chopping, piercing and killing that were essential for everyday existence. The beauty of flint lay in its newly mined properties. Fresh from the chalk it has the consistency of hard toffee, broken and flaked with practised ease using soft antler hammers. The presence of valuable flint must have been obvious to early communities. Any pit dug into the chalk was likely to produce the odd nodule, while observations of the chalk faces of the seaward cliffs of the Downs would have revealed thick seams of flint. Prehistoric people, of course, were not geologists or natural scientists. They were, however, deeply conscious of their dependence on the living plants and animals around them, and no doubt believed in forces beyond themselves, such as ancestors or spirits, who controlled all the materials they relied upon for life. The quality of the tabular flint, at such a depth in the chalk, would have seemed like the casual gift of a capricious spirit. To retrieve the prize would have required dangerously deep digging, tunnelling and mining, while hoping that the ancestors and spirits of the underworld would provide protection.

In the chalk cliffs of Beachy Head and below Belle Tout you can see horizontal lines of tabular flint, prized by prehistoric flint miners, and layers of nodular flint.

However, to begin at the very beginning, the first wet footprints in the muddy earth in the South Downs National Park are associated with earlier buried chalk cliff lines and beaches that border the southern line of the chalk Downs, from Brighton to Portsdown in Hampshire. Some of these early cliffs, now inland, were formed half a million years ago, when sea levels were much higher. A remarkable glimpse into that very different world comes from Boxgrove (Walk 8). Here members of several meat-eating families (from an ancestral human species to ourselves) took time to make beautiful oval flint handaxes which they then used to butcher large mammals such as horses, giant deer, rhinoceroses, bears and bison. They were capable of organised hunting, perhaps using spears of some sort, and, in the absence of fire, may have eaten the meat raw. A fragment of human leg bone found at the site shows that these individuals must have been strong-limbed. They were living at the far extremity of human occupation at the time and intermittently retreated southwards when the climate cooled.

Flint was extremely important to the first hunters and gatherers who began to venture up on to the Downs from around 6000 BCE onwards, with the general warming of the climate following at the end of the last Ice Age. These people (the same species as ourselves) probably comprised small bands of several families. They hunted deer, wild cattle and pigs, and trapped birds and rodents. They caught fish, collected shellfish, dug up roots and tubers, and gathered nuts and berries. They fashioned garments from skins, baskets from plant fibres and erected shelters from branches and saplings. They probably moved around from seasonal camp to camp. Fundamental to all these activities was a complex toolkit made of axes and differently shaped small pieces of flint, with keenly serrated edges – archaeologists call these microliths. Their campsites have been found the length and breadth of the South Downs National Park, from Bullock Down (behind Beachy Head) in the east to West Heath (between Petersfield and Midhurst) and Selborne (in the north of the Park). Combinations of microliths may have been glued with birch resin (a black tar-like substance obtained from burning birch bark) into wooden handles, making the first composite tools.

From around 4000 BCE farming lifestyles, based on the cultivation of cereals and the raising of cattle and sheep, gradually replaced and marginalised hunting and gathering. Flint was important to the first farmers of what is now the South Downs National Park, but some of it was extracted in a wholly different way. Unlike their hunter predecessors, who had obtained flint from small pits, surface scatters, beach cobbles or river gravels, the first farmers mined the deeply layered flint, leaving a series of remarkable mine shafts, underground galleries, spoil dumps and working areas at several sites in West Sussex, such as Harrow Hill, Church Hill, Long Down and Cissbury (Walks 6 & 8). The mines seem to have been excavated using picks fashioned from deer antlers and shovels made from their shoulder blades, and the flint from them was largely used for the manufacture of axes, perhaps for the purpose of clearing trees for fields or for exchange with neighbouring communities. Despite the better quality of mined flint, there is plenty of circumstantial evidence to suggest that the dangerous deep mining of flint may have had a social and ritual significance, as well as a functional motivation. Enigmatic chalk objects and incised lines on the walls of some galleries, plus occasional human burials and individual human bones, coupled with the fact that surface flint was readily available, argue that there was something in the very prestige of this difficult task that encouraged people to excavate. The scale of mining was small and episodic; perhaps only one or two shafts were open at any one time. However, the occurrence of paired shafts raises the possibility that occasional flint mining was a ritualised and competitive practice. In addition, there may have been something prized in the very colour of mined flint. The quest between competing kin groups may have been more important than the buried quarry.

The materials of chalk and flint are very different. You can saw, cleave and sometimes carve chalk into manageable blocks, but the stone itself is soft, porous and weathers easily. Some of the harder chalks, occasionally referred to as clunch, can be used for internal walls not exposed to weathering. An important characteristic of chalk, thanks to all those billions of dead plankton, is that it is alkaline, making it an ideal material to reduce the acidity of some soils, breaking up heavy clay soils

At the western end of Cissbury hill fort you can still see the filled-in shafts of flint mines some 6,000 years old. The later hill-fort bank is in the middle of the image, running from left to right.

A street in Arundel illustrating the use of horizontal rows of pebble flints on the external walls. Brick quoins form the right-angled corners.

and allowing manure to penetrate more effectively, and thus making them more fertile. Flint, on the other hand, can be flaked into flat or sharp shapes, although it can snap and break; otherwise it is water resistant and durable, and well suited for use in external walls and foundations. Most or all of these qualities were probably known to people throughout prehistory. It is not surprising, therefore, that those master builders the Romans, who constructed most of the earliest stone buildings or at least stone foundations in southern Britain, realised the different building materials on offer in the South Downs National Park. At Fishbourne Roman Palace, constructed in the late first century CE, the foundations comprised layered and mortared courses of roughly squared flint, with facing stones from the local greensand, quarried from north of the South Downs where it occurred in a line from Bignor through Petersfield. Chalk was conspicuous by its absence.

Throughout the South Downs National Park many important medieval and later buildings were constructed from combinations of local building stone: flint, greensand, chalk and occasionally other varieties of sandstone. Randomly shaped 'boulder' flints can simply be laid in irregular patterns to make field boundary walls, while rounded cobble flints can be mortared in neat horizontal rows. Knapped and squared flint can be used for facing stones, sometimes forming startling patterns like the chequerboard façade of the medieval building of Marlipins, Shoreham, or deployed to stylish effect as in the eighteenth-century two-storey stables at Goodwood House. Flint was not good for making corners, and these were often managed through the use of squared greensand or building stone from the Isle of Wight or imported from Caen in Normandy. Chalk was much more frequently used as the internal rubble make-up of walls or for their inside facing. In the north of the Park, around Selborne, a belt of greensand, known locally as malmstone, is accessible and can be seen in the façades of many buildings, formed by regular or irregular courses of this creamy-coloured stone (Walk 14). Brick and tile, dug, moulded and baked from the clays of the Weald, gradually complemented stonework from the sixteenth century onwards. Only a minority of buildings were made of stone, of course. Humbler buildings utilised clays for cob-and-daub walls, timber for roof purlins and furniture, and dried grasses for roofing thatch.

The earth thus provided tools for our earliest ancestors and, more recently, stones and organic materials for buildings, roofs, furniture, utensils, containers, gates and fences. But wandering through the South Downs National Park you will stumble on tell-tale signs of how the earth has provided the ingredients that helped other vitally important processes. The white gash of an old chalk quarry, particularly along the north scarp of the Downs at places like Amberley Chalk Pits, is testimony to the extraction of chalk not only for building but also for quantities of lime for use in construction, especially from the eighteenth century onwards. Chalk can also be burnt in kilns to produce lime to assist agricultural fertility (Walk 7). Farms often had their own kiln in the corner of a field built for that purpose. The north scarp of the Downs is occasionally scarred diagonally by deep cuts that run down its flank, providing the trackways or 'bostals' for the movement of chalk, lime and animals (Walk 10).

The remains of the recent past can be just as moving as those from earlier times. The abandoned Beeding Cement Works, once a major employer making cement from the local chalk, now lies eerily quiet, its austere façades pierced by rows of broken windows. Finally, across the South Downs National Park extensive coppiced woodlands provided vital fuel for the production of charcoal, used in the Wealden iron industries in the sixteenth to eighteenth centuries, by itinerant charcoal burners. Making charcoal in makeshift kilns was a slow and unpredictable process, sometimes lasting up to five days, and occasionally leading to rapid deforestation when no replacement plantings were made. But for the charcoal burner, in his hut, the long nights tending the fire resulted in a commodity that others would pay for.

The earth of the South Downs National Park therefore provided some of the raw materials with which generations of communities could provide homes and furniture, tools and fuel. But the mainstay of existence – food, drink and clothing – conjured up from the natural resources of the area remained a constant preoccupation, from those first families at Boxgrove to the twenty-first century. Let's look for some tell-tale signs people have left behind in their constant quest to stay fed, watered and warm.

HUNTING, FISHING, FARMING AND CONSERVATION

The archaeological evidence for diet is slight and often uncertain, and we need to use our imaginations to put flesh on the bone, so to speak. As the climate warmed some 8,000 years ago, a patchy woodland of oak, hazel, lime, ash and elm spread throughout the area now designated as the South Downs National Park, and it was into this kind of environment that the first bands of hunters and gatherers, groups of several families, set up seasonal camps. They may have used flint axes and fires to open up and enlarge natural clearances in the scrub and woodland, thereby attracting grazing animals such as deer, perhaps fed with ivy by the hunters, wild boar and wild cattle. At Iping Common in West Sussex, on the greensand, pollen evidence recovered from an excavation suggests deliberate opening up of a hazel woodland to establish clearings of heather-covered heathland (Walk 9). Hunted animals provided not only protein but also bones for tools, skins for clothing and containers, and sinews for cordage. The only truly domesticated animals were dogs, no doubt employed to help with hunting and fetching quarry. Other foods came in the form of nuts, berries, wild grasses and fungi; hazelnuts were particularly favoured. Fishing and shellfish complemented the diet.

Studies of surviving hunters and gatherers in other parts of the world have provided some useful stimuli for our imaginations, although we must be wary of over-generalisation. What they do show is that hunters and gatherers in our area may have been self-sufficient with only a few hours of 'work' per day; that they may have been quite egalitarian, with no fixed leaders and few material goods, with women undertaking most of the gathering and men doing the hunting. The studies also point to small groups of people who had an intensively knowledgeable appreciation of all the living things in their environment, who knew both how to manage them and, most importantly, to sustain resources for the future. Their relationship with the landscape, and with the things that grew and lived there,

Hazelnuts, seemingly one of the staple foods of the early hunters and gatherers on the Downs. But the humble hazel has many uses.

was probably overridingly mystical, as is suggested by the ceremonial deer masks found at the broadly contemporary site of Star Carr in North Yorkshire. They were part of nature, not above it. However, we must be wary of portraying our early ancestors as happy bands of wandering and well-fed environmentalists. There were, no doubt, plenty of quarrels and disputes, occasional inter-band aggression, seasonal food shortages and a life expectancy much shorter than our own.

The fundamentals of diet gradually changed around 6,000 years ago, beginning with the arrival of some groups of people, and some new-fangled ideas, from the near Continent. They brought with them the resources for rudimentary farming – domesticated animals such as cattle, sheep, goat and pig, and cereals – and the first cooking vessels. Larger clearances were made on the Downs by the newcomers, but for a long time, perhaps more than 2,000 years, the landscape of the Downs would have been a mosaic of woodland and seasonally cleared grasslands for pasture and planting. At Bishopstone, at the eastern extremity of the South Downs National Park, evidence has been found for prehistoric ancestors of modern cereals, such as emmer wheat and six-row barley, as well as possible food plants like fat hen, burdock and chickweed. Shellfish collecting continued, with mussels, oysters, cockles and limpets in abundance.

Again, it's time to use our imagination. How did these newcomers relate to the indigenous hunters and gatherers? Studies elsewhere suggest that, although these lifestyles are very different, hunters and farmers can exist in proximity and usefully exchange products and services that each group is more skilled at acquiring. They can also intermarry, leading to socially intertwined relationships as well as 'economic' ones. Without taking the analogy too far, you might imagine that the patchwork of woodlands for hunting and gathering, and farmed, seasonal clearances might symbolise the social arrangements of communities of hunters and farmers living in close proximity. That closeness, however, may have brought its own problems of misunderstandings, petty thefts, trespass, animal rustling or worse.

Over the long term, there is something inherently unstable in the relationship between ways of life dependent on hunting and those reliant on farming, although farmers often still engaged in hunting, especially in times of food shortages. Recent colonial history demonstrates the rapid marginalisation of those Native Americans or Australian Aborigines who relied exclusively on hunting, gathering and fishing. While the transition in our region was nowhere near as rapid, eventually the gradual restrictions placed on hunting and gathering by the growing numbers of farmers, improving agricultural technology and the larger size of their herds and clearings would have led inexorably to an accelerating reduction in the 'wild' landscapes left for hunting and gathering. The archaeological evidence is both clear and dramatic: the first permanent rectangular fields, surrounded by hedges and banks, appeared on the Downs some 3,500 years ago. Two enclosures at New Barn Down, on the block of downland between the Arun and the Adur, are linked to a system of rectangular fields and trackways. An animal or storage structure and a quern stone remind us of the farming necessity of storing harvested produce to feed both animals and humans over the winter. Another example of the permanence of farming settlements and their fields is the complex at Plumpton, where field systems stretch south-east from the main centre of habitation. It is a wonderful place to visit, with views south-east towards the sea, and the north escarpment and Wealden views a short walk away. Finally, the southern flanks of Butser Hill, just south of Petersfield in Hampshire, are covered with an impressive network of prehistoric rectangular fields, seen clearly from the air as a lattice of boundary earthworks, or lynchets.

Climate change, so threatening for the contemporary world, has occurred before. The onset of the Iron Age, about 700 BCE, coincided with a much damper environment, further intensifying the environmental pressures on farming communities. Such were the consequences that population numbers may have shrunk for a few generations as increased rainfall, soil erosion and flooding rivers made some land unusable. The surviving downland communities that emerged from this disaster invested in protection, not only for themselves but for their herds and agricultural surpluses. A four-post timber structure at Park Brow, just north of Cissbury Ring, set amongst fields, may have been a small granary. Surrounded by a protected landscape of palisades, fields and trackways, finds of spindle whorls, loom weights and a weaving comb, attest the need to keep warm and dry. A settlement further west above Chichester at Lavant, guarded by the nearby hill fort of the Trundle, contained round buildings, an iron sickle and a series of four-post granaries for storage.

An agricultural revolution occurred when the area now occupied by the South Downs National Park was incorporated into the Roman Empire. New foods

The Bronze Age settlement at Plumpton Plain. The complex of earthworks and trackways form a rare survival in a landscape heavily utilised for agriculture in recent centuries.

arrived with Roman administration, and new tableware with which to serve them. There were classic Mediterranean imports such as figs, olives and grapes. Additionally, novel fruits and vegetables were introduced and became integrated into the local agricultural system, such as domestic apples, pears, plums, cherries, walnuts, lettuce and leeks. However, it was not all good news for the conquered. The Romans introduced taxation on a widespread scale – both in agricultural kind and in cash. As a result, new field systems proliferated (e.g., at Thundersbarrow above Shoreham and at Jevington in the east of the Park) and greater yields were demanded from older prehistoric fields (Walk 5). A corn-drying oven at Bullock Down, near Eastbourne, two corn-drying kilns at Thundersbarrow and no less than eleven such kilns attached to an aisled barn at West Blatchington in Hove indicate the pressure on farmers to increase outputs.

The collapse of the Roman Empire meant that market-orientated agricultural practices disappeared. Population declined and subsequently Saxon newcomers settled amongst the surviving locals in the South Downs, sometimes living in one place for a few generations then relocating (as at Chalton in Hampshire). They mostly practised subsistence farming geared towards feeding local kin rather than producing a surplus for exchange. At Bishopstone, near Newhaven in East Sussex, cereals were grown on fields attached to the settlement, while animals included sheep, cattle, pig, horse, red and roe deer, geese and fowl. Bones from conger eel and whiting show that resources from the sea were also not ignored. These settler societies had simple, subsistence concerns, as the few finds of whetstones, spindle whorls and pottery from a typical rectangular sunken hut at North Marden (north of Chichester) indicate. However, towards the end of the Saxon period, the impact of Christianity and the growth of aristocratic estates, both secular and religious, led to the rise of high-status settlements founded in new locations. Again at Bishopstone, but this time founded close to the extant Saxon church, a cemetery and then a privileged settlement developed. The inhabitants fed on pig and marine fish, as well as red deer, roe deer, hare and badger. Land organisation and agricultural tributes from those who worked the land were designed to support conspicuous consumption and 'hospitality feasting' by those at the summit of local social hierarchies.

By the Norman Conquest of 1066 the Sussex half of the South Downs National Park was divided into administrative areas known as 'rapes'. There were six in all, each controlled by a castle, such as Arundel, Bramber and Lewes (Walk 2). They formed the foundations of a feudal system of lay and ecclesiastical estates for exploiting the labour of peasant farmers, as evidenced by the size of the Benedictine Barn at Alciston. The downland landscape was home to a mosaic of economic practices, from extensive sheep pastures (more common in the east), some open fields, aristocratic forests, deer parks for hunting (more common in the west, like that at Marwell where plentiful trees facilitated both the observation of deer and concealment of the stalker), rabbit warrens (bred for their fur and meat) and the consumption of high-status foods from the sea or closer-to-home fishponds (Walk 14). The ubiquity of sheep farming on the Downs in the medieval period was closely linked to the cultivation of fields. A three-course rotation was often employed of autumn wheat, spring barley and fallow. Sheep, kept largely for their wool, were looked after by solitary downland shepherds during the summer and used as moveable manure heaps to fertilise the crop-yielding soils at night. Hazel stands, coppiced on a seven-year cycle, supplied the portable hurdles for managing large flocks.

Throughout the last 1,000 years the Park landscape was shaped by social and political changes taking place on the national and international stages. The slow erosion of the manorial system of farming, with peasants tied to the land of their lords, the emergence of parishes, the break-up of large ecclesiastical estates following the English Reformation of the sixteenth century and the success of the iron-making revolution in the nearby Weald radically changed ways of life. The onset of more 'rational' ways to farm, inspired by the Enlightenment of the eighteenth century and the emergence of large, industrialised cities, also opened up new opportunities. Wealthy aristocrats constructed 'great houses' (Walks 1 & 7) complemented by large estates (especially in the western section of the Park). Inspired by the age of 'scientific' discoveries, they brought fresh ideas to downland farming. Innovative fodder crops for sheep, such as swedes and turnips, imported initially from the Continent, were planted. A famous improved brand of sheep was bred on the Downs, the Southdown. Celebrated for its quality of wool, it was claimed that live wool on the back of a sheep in the morning could be tailored into a gentleman's coat by the evening. The growing industries elsewhere in the country, and the masses of workers required by them, eventually led to a greater demand for meat from sheep.

The twentieth century also brought significant changes to downland life. Political ideologies and two world wars impoverished most of the great country houses, leading to the breaking up of many remaining estates and the ploughing of

The sensuous profile of Wolstonbury Hill projects northwards to provide a fine vantage point over the Weald (Walk 4).

A view towards Harrow Hill (top left) across a field of rape. Note the alternating leaf colour of the line of trees sloping downwards towards Lee Farm (Walk 6).

more extensive areas of downland to feed a post-1945 population living off rations. Mechanisation in farming led to rural depopulation and the post-war creation of large downland fenced fields, covered in cereals or other crops, presented the casual visitor with a more restricted landscape and undermined earlier attempts to create a National Park. However, the emergence of middle-class tourism brought new visitors to admire the sweeping downland scenery, and the momentum for recognition of the special qualities of this landscape gathered renewed pace.

But it is time to retrace our steps. Having looked at how people obtained food, drink and clothing from the territory of the Park, we now want to see what kinds of buildings they constructed to shelter themselves from the elements and, importantly, how they sometimes used them to show off their status to the neighbours.

LIVING BUILDINGS

The archaeology of buildings doesn't have a great deal to tell us for the earliest part of human occupation in the South Downs National Park. The last hunters and gatherers, who camped on the Downs between 6,000 and 8,000 years ago, discarded flint tools but left no traces of their dwellings (or at least none that have been discovered yet). From evidence elsewhere, the circular or oval structures would have been made of wood and covered with organic material such as skins. Part of the reason for their non-discovery is that they would have been relatively flimsy since they were designed to be not only lived in but carried, too, from seasonal camp to camp. Nor do we have much better luck when we look for the houses of the first farmers on the Downs, who grazed their cattle and planted crops from 4000 BCE onwards. Again, by analogy elsewhere archaeologists should have found at least one or two rectangular timber buildings, their wooden posts rotting and leaving post-holes in the ground. There should be long-houses, for extended families, and perhaps byres for animals or storage, especially as the South Downs National Park is one of the richest areas for other types of monument constructed by the early agriculturalists. These buildings lie hidden somewhere, but where? Some people argue that they lie concealed at the bottom of valley sides, underneath metres of agriculturally disturbed soil washed down through the ages.

The earliest domestic structures that lie within the South Downs National Park appear associated with the first signs of intensification of farming, represented by the small, rectangular fields, dating to around 3,500 years ago. Small, round, timber buildings, with wattle-and-daub walls and thatch roofs cluster together in downland farmsteads, often surrounded by palisades or embankments. Let's look at two excavated examples, Black Patch and Itford Hill, to the east of Lewes. At Black Patch a number of circular huts were discovered associated with an extensive system of fields. The huts were constructed on terraces levelled into the sloping hillside. Five huts were excavated, along with nearby fence lines and ponds. Artefacts within the huts suggest that some were used for sleeping in, others for flint knapping, lambing or storage. The social structure of the occupants is notoriously difficult to reconstruct from archaeological remains but it is possible that polygamy was practised and some of the huts were for ancillary wives. Alternatively, they could have been for siblings or grandparents. Itford Hill is similar to Black Patch, sited on a southward-facing downland slope, with fields to the south. The latest interpretation of the site suggests that the settlement started with two houses, which expanded to five, then shrank to three and finally two. It is very tempting to think that these fluctuations mirror the number of family residents, swelling as children are young, shrinking as they grow to adults, find partners and leave, perhaps to found their own settlement. Similar farmsteads have been excavated at Plumpton Plain and further west at New Barn Down, above Worthing. In Hampshire an extensive area of unenclosed occupation was revealed at Easton Lane, near Winchester. Here, ten circular post-built structures were found, along with numerous other buildings, pits, ditches and burials. Other potentially contemporary sites are suggested for Chalton and West Meon.

During the much wetter Iron Age, from 700 BCE, circular timber houses, perhaps slightly larger, were the main house type. The best example from Sussex is near Lavant, at a site called Chalkpit Lane. An unenclosed southward-facing settlement of up to thirteen round-houses, complete with four-, six- and eight-post granaries, was excavated. There were some rudimentary indications of planning at Chalkpit Lane, with the houses seemingly distributed either side of a communal open space, facing each other. The other interesting thing about this site is that the settlement boundary was not located and it is conceivable that there is an extensive complex of round-houses, perhaps thirty or more, at this location, just south of the Trundle hill fort. At Winnall Down, near Winchester, eight circular structures and other features were surrounded by a bank and ditch.

What was it like to live in a round-house? Luckily you can visit Butser Ancient Farm, just south of Petersfield, and look around one of these houses yourself. For the modern visitor there are often two concerns: the lack of privacy and the 'smoke gets in your eyes' problem. In a large round-house, with effectively only one large round room (although screens could be put up to at least provide visual privacy), how could you do anything 'in private'? The key to answering this issue lies in realising that our concept of 'privacy' is a very modern one. In the ancient world, for instance, domestic slaves often slept in the same bedroom as their masters and mistresses. Visitors always ask about cooking over hearths in the centre of round-houses, and the fact that no round-house has a chimney. In practice, the smoke from a central fire curls gently upwards to the conical roof, and slowly escapes through the thatch, killing lots of little bugs as it does and thereby prolonging the lifespan of the house. Many of these late prehistoric round-houses faced south-east, towards the rising sun, probably both for religious and functional reasons. Imagine the light streaming in through the door in the early morning,

A reconstruction of an Iron Age round-house from Butser. The wattle-and-daub walls and thatched roof, plus the central hearth within, make for a surprisingly warm interior.

lighting up the southern sides of the house and moving around the walls towards the north in the early afternoon. The daily journey of reflected sunlight on the internal wall of the round-house mirrored the travel of the sun across the sky, emphasising the cyclical aspects of rural lives.

Fundamental changes in living buildings occurred when the Park region and southern Britain were incorporated into the Roman Empire. While most people continued to live in round-houses, a few adopted new ways of living in rectangular buildings, some of which, in the countryside, are described by archaeologists, rather grandly, as 'villas'. You can visit an excellent reconstruction of part of a villa (one that was excavated at Sparsholt, near Winchester) at Butser. The differences between this structure and the round-houses are obvious. The tiled roof, lime-washed walls and windows are all things that don't feature in circular houses. But the really big differences lie within. There are several separate rectangular rooms of varying sizes (allowing status differences to emerge between the inhabitants), a flanking corridor and a hypocaust (under-floor heating system); many villas also had communal baths. You don't have to be an archaeologist to imagine the different attitudes of the people who lived in villas. They were interested in making a statement about their status, enjoyed some degree of privacy and had novel attitudes about decorated floors and the use of hot water for bathing, as evidenced from surviving villas at Fishbourne and Bignor. They also may have owned slaves,

One of the central images from the first mosaic found at Bignor Roman Villa in the early nineteenth century. A youthful Ganymede is carried from Mount Ida to be a cupbearer to the gods.

who, in some cases, slept in traditional round-houses, no doubt located discreetly to the rear of the main building.

By the end of the Roman period, while Roman towns such as Chichester and Winchester were in decline, some villas in the countryside witnessed their greatest period of prosperity. You can see for yourself just how grand some villas had become by visiting Bignor Roman Villa, south of Petworth on the fertile greensand ridge in the shadow of the north scarp. In its final form, the villa consisted of some sixty-five rooms surrounding a courtyard, with a number of outlying farm buildings. The latest phase of building involved additions to the north wing, and it is here that most of the fine mosaics are located. The reconstruction of the façade of an aisled barn at Meonstoke shows just how sophisticated some agricultural buildings had also become. The collapse of the western Roman Empire brought those lifestyles to an end. The economic infrastructure that supported monetary exchange for building products and craft workers who designed and laid elaborate mosaics slowly disintegrated. Security in the countryside disappeared and Saxon newcomers took full advantage. The next living buildings to appear in the South Downs National Park went back to basics.

Saxons migrating to Sussex from northern Europe brought with them the tradition of thatched timber building. Two types of structure predominate in these early villages: rectangular buildings used for occupation and small sunken-floored huts that were probably used for a variety of craft activities, including weaving. These types of settlements have been found along the length of the South Downs National Park, from Bishopstone in the east, to Botolphs by the river Adur, West Marden north of Chichester, Chalton on the Hampshire Downs and Shavards Farm, Meonstoke (Walk 13). There is a concentration of early Saxon finds between the rivers Ouse and Cuckmere, and it is possible that the late Romano-British people granted lands here to the Saxons in return for tribute or services of some kind. However, equally early Saxon graves have been found at Eastbourne. Some of the Saxons were not averse to living in the decaying ruins of Roman villas, like Beddingham, near Lewes. Other families must have been quite fearful as they wandered past crumbling Roman buildings, noting the tumbled stone walls and gaping roofs, spaces now colonised by animals, birds and, no doubt at night, ghosts.

By the later Saxon period population growth and an increasing diversity of economic practices, including exchange and trade with the near Continent, led to the emergence of different settlement types. At Botolphs, in the Adur valley, rectangular timber buildings, on east–west and north–south alignments, were built over the early Saxon settlement (Walk 5). At Bishopstone, the late Saxon settlement buildings, this time on a different site to their early Saxon predecessor but with the same orientations as Botolphs, were laid out to the north of a Christian shrine and early church. They included a remarkable cellared structure that probably supported a tower, suggesting a distinctly high-status site in the countryside. During this period, in the tenth and eleventh centuries, the Park's first towns (since the Romans left, that is) were being founded. Steyning, near the Adur north of the Downs, and Winchester, in the west, are two of the foremost examples (both just outside the Park's boundaries), along with the *burh* underneath modern Lewes established in the time of King Alfred. Rows of rectangular buildings and newly laid streets, along with evidence of metalworking and the minting of coins, reveal embryonic urban elements in a still dominantly rural landscape.

The new Norman overlords were intent on maximising the tax returns from the countryside, either in kind or coin, as that nationwide tax assessment document, Domesday Book, indicates. Both the settlements in the countryside which formed villages and nascent urban sites around new Norman castles continued to grow in numbers. Indeed, the thirteenth century saw a period of expansion when marginal land within the South Downs National Park was taken over for farming and the establishment of small villages. However, a combination of several factors, including the emparkment of land for hunting by the rich landowners and the Black Death of the mid-fourteenth century, led to the desertion of hundreds of these outlying villages, forming the phenomenon that archaeologists call Deserted Medieval Villages. Often these comprised no more than a single street, with timbered and thatched buildings either side, a small church and perhaps a manor house and a mill. You can still walk along the deserted and grassed streets, and over the small rectangular house plots, of some of these pioneering agriculturalists. Abandoned villages were once populated at Perching, above Southwick; at Monkton, north of Chichester; Abbotstone, near New Alresford; Beddingham, near Lewes; and further examples existed at Colemore and Priors Dean in East Hampshire. In some cases it is tempting to conjure up an idyll of rural life, but in reality, under the watchful eyes of the Lord of the Manor's bailiff, the daily grind must have been long and hard.

At the other end of the social scale, the break-up of large ecclesiastical estates such as those of Lewes Priory and the Bishop of Winchester – the latter one of the wealthiest in England – during the Reformation, and their sale by the Crown into private hands, provided opportunities for the elite to build grand country houses, often surrounded by hunting parks and landscaped gardens. The larger aristocratic houses are concentrated in the middle section of the South Downs National Park and include such properties as Uppark, Stansted and Wiston (walk 7). One of the grandest is Petworth House, rebuilt in 1688 by Charles Seymour, 6th Duke of Somerset, and altered in the 1870s by Anthony Salvin. The site was previously occupied by a fortified manor house founded by Henry de Percy, the thirteenth-century chapel and undercroft of which still survive. In the east, lesser large houses, those of the well-off gentry, included Danny and Plumpton. The majority of these houses were of two or three storeys, often laid out in an 'E'- or 'H'-shaped plan. The Hampshire village of Chawton is famous for having both Chawton House, an Elizabethan manor house and home to Jane Austen's brother Edward Knight, and a large seventeenth-century house where Jane Austen herself spent the last eight years of her life. Many of these grand homes survived into the nineteenth and early twentieth centuries, from time to time hosting the highest

Jane Austen's brick-built house at Chawton in the north of the Park. She spent her last eight years here, writing *Mansfield Park, Emma* and *Persuasion* within these walls.

echelons of society (Edward VII enjoyed West Dean enough to make several visits). These large estates were also home to hundreds of estate workers and their families, who sometimes lived in purpose-built accommodation on site and spent their entire lives as part of the estate community. Relations, and occasional tensions, between the estate aristocracy and its workers are now, of course, the stuff of televised English costume dramas.

The living buildings of the modern period comprise a mix of old and new. In the towns within the South Downs National Park older timber-framed medieval houses were provided with a Georgian make-over, with emphasis on a frontage pierced by evenly spaced windows, providing an overall geometric effect (Walk 12). The rising numbers of the middle class constructed fine Victorian and Edwardian houses lining suburban streets. Not everyone wanted to show off, however. A victim of Victorian celebrity culture, the poet Tennyson hid his house on the slopes of Black Down (Walk 11). The new wealth of industrial entrepreneurs spawned enterprises in the countryside that needed numbers of workers to turn a profit. The more enlightened, perhaps more canny, operators built rows of workers' cottages close by, ensuring that if workers were late, they could be easily found. An example of such housing was built at Tidemills, east of Newhaven, and on the Glynde estate, near Lewes. In Hampshire, in the late nineteenth century, the gin merchant William Nicholson built a lot of properties in and around Privett for his workers at the Basing Park Estate. The consistent architectural form and style of Nicholson's buildings is what gives Privett its individual character, which included gables, flint with brick dressings and decorative stones such as Nicholson's own crest and initials.

Rising population numbers in the twentieth century meant that the need for new, lower-cost housing was paramount, much as it still is today. The settlement of Peacehaven, on the chalk downs some 9.7km (6 miles) east of Brighton, was a novel, and controversial, planned town in the 1920s. A grid of roads (running east–west) and avenues (north–south) created plots for some relatively poor housing, occasionally fashioned from ex-army huts or old railway carriages. Notwithstanding its controversial beginning, Peacehaven has contributed in its own way to the history of the area, if only by serving as a warning about the dangers of poorly designed buildings – hence its location just outside the Park. It now supports a flourishing local history society, and has notably featured in recent literature and drama, including *Brighton Rock*, *Mr Bean* and *Eastenders*.

Living buildings provide shelter and warmth and their diverse characters, materials and history provide an obvious reminder of past livelihoods within the South Downs National Park. However, people are instinctively social, and there is little doubt that they were equally so in remote prehistory, quite likely even more so. And much of social and communal life takes place outdoors. The first great gathering places were marked out on the Downs nearly 6,000 years ago. It's time to travel back and find out what they were talking about.

MEETING PLACES, MEETING PEOPLE

Ever since the first people arrived in our area they met other people from time to time, and gathered together in larger groups. It is easy to think that these occasional gatherings were prompted by the need to co-operate in some functional activity. For instance, some 8,000 years ago hunters and gatherers may have banded together to clear patches of woodland or to organise themselves so that they could more easily stalk a herd of deer and perhaps drive one into an ambush where it could be killed. The resulting amount of meat, far too large for a small family to consume, could be shared out amongst the wider group. But there were other, more sociable, reasons why people occasionally concentrated in one place. They could exchange information, seek out partners, conduct a variety of rituals relating to life-cycle events, such as births, coming-of-age ceremonies, marriages, deaths, give and receive gifts, share out food, feast and party, decide on questions of right and wrong, compete for status and group approval, gamble and drink, or just discuss the weather. In many ways these are some of the things that we still do today when we go to meeting places.

The places where hunters and gatherers congregated to tell stories around camp fires have not survived for us to see today. Archaeological finds, however, demonstrate that plenty of them would have sat around cooking hearths on the greensand ridge, to the north of the chalk scarp, or the heathlands of the Rother valley. A combination of light woodland, hazel trees and especially nuts, and well-drained sandy soils made them ideal locations for seasonal or permanent camps.

But you can visit some of the meeting places of the very first farmers within the South Downs National Park, who began to manage the landscape for cattle and sheep, and for crops. These were the direct but distant ancestors of downland farmers today. These meeting places are described by archaeologists as 'causewayed camps' and most date to around 6,000 years ago. They are found on the Sussex Downs (as well as elsewhere in England), but there is no known example (yet) in the Hampshire section of the South Downs National Park, including the greensand areas. These places must have been built by the first farmers who came from the near Continent, bringing livestock and cereals with them. They are circular monuments, defining spaces some 200m or more in diameter. Their boundaries, often concentric, are formed by banks and ditches through which there are many 'causeways', hence the name. They were often built in places where there had been no previous human activity, suggesting these were neutral or special places, distant from where people ordinarily lived. Examples in Sussex include the Trundle (above Chichester), Barkhale on the north scarp near Bignor Hill, Whitehawk (above Brighton) and Combe Hill (above Eastbourne) (Walk 3). In Hampshire a small circle of pits was discovered and excavated at Winnall Down (just east of Winchester). The pits contained four red deer antlers, some pieces of pottery and flint flakes. This site could also have functioned as an early meeting place, but is quite dissimilar to the causewayed camps further east.

What took place at these meeting places? The broken pieces of pottery and artefacts, and fragments of animal and human bones found in some of the ditches of these 'camps' can be interpreted in many different ways. Some people have

The Devil's Humps above Kingley Vale, near Chichester. Fine examples of Bronze Age burial mounds, and really nice places today to sit and admire the scenery.

suggested that each of the separate sections of ditches, divided by causeways, were in some way owned by a particular family or kin group. The activities that have been proposed for the meeting places range from feasting to making and exchanging artefacts, from carrying out rituals to occasional human burials. Just as important, if not more so, were activities like those outlined at the start of this section, which have left behind no archaeological traces. These sites were special as places but they were also special at certain times of the agricultural year. It is quite probable that the leaders of communities only allowed these gatherings to take place at specified times, for instance in late summer after any crops had been harvested or before winter when surplus young cattle were sacrificed and consumed.

Meeting places changed location and form from century to century. The great number of burial monuments within the South Downs National Park – the earthen mounds called 'long barrows' and 'round barrows' – provided particular places where people congregated, not only in the act of burial itself but also, subsequently, to commune with the dead and ask protection from the ancestors, as well as communicate with one another (Walk 3). There are also some hints that certain settlement locations could also function as meeting places. Just to the north of the 3,000-year-old settlement of Itford Hill (near Lewes) was an isolated circular timber structure, quite possibly roofed, with an entrance to the south. Inside, under a pile of flint, lay the cremated remains of an old man, and outside were the cremated remains of at least eleven men, women and children. This looks like the grave of the man who founded the adjacent settlement, and the descendants of a number of such settlements could have met here to honour their founding father. Roughly contemporary with Itford is a very distinctive enclosure on Highdown Hill, near Worthing. It stands apart and seemingly in front of the main chalk ridge of the Downs, making it an obvious landmark for those further along the coast or approaching from the sea. Bronze axes, chisels, knives and a gold ring found at Highdown show that one of the prominent activities at this meeting place was exchange.

This exchange was probably more akin to our own custom of giving presents on particular occasions, rather than acquiring new stuff through payment in kind. People at meeting places both gave and received things, sometimes even before they talked. In many cultures the act of exchange, between strangers who may not even share a language, is the first act of communication, of making a possible foe a probable friend. In the prehistoric period it is quite likely that social ties between people of different communities were cemented through receiving objects from their neighbours. When they took gifts back to their homes, they took with them something of the giver, both materially and spiritually. The meeting places of the Iron Age in the South Downs National Park were undoubtedly the great hill forts dotted along the chalk ridge, from St Catherine's Hill east of Winchester (Walk 15) to Hollingbury above Brighton (Walk 1). Within these encircling earthen banks, people congregated from time to time, giving agricultural tribute to their chiefs and spiritual leaders – the Druids – conducting rituals and sacrifices, giving

The town walls of Roman Chichester protected the town's inhabitants and buildings. Town life was an essential component of the Roman way of life.

and receiving gifts, adjudicating between rights and wrongs, and bartering live-stock and perhaps slaves. The vital social glue, however, that underpinned all these activities, and made people feel that they belonged to a community, was the sharing of the significant and the trivial: how to perform a proper sacrifice or how to address a chief; gathering together to witness significant performances; indulging in gossip, shows of affection, spiteful rumours, competitive trials of strength and fortune-telling.

When southern Britain was incorporated into the Roman Empire the new administrators tried to encourage an urban way of living amongst some of the local population. Towns were founded at Winchester and Chichester, as were smaller settlements such as Neatham, near Alton – all just outside the Park. The meeting places in these towns were known by the Latin word *forum* (pl. *fora*). At such places justice could be administered, disputes resolved, taxes collected, goods traded and bought, and both local and Roman gods honoured. But most of the population were not of continental origin and could trace their origin back to forebears in the Iron Age. It is not surprising, therefore, that a number of rural shrines were founded, such as at Lancing and Bow Hill (above Chichester), where local gods could still receive sacrifices, and some of these were even sited within the ancient hill forts (Walk 7). A detached polygonal building close to Stroud Roman Villa at Petersfield may be an example from Hampshire.

Under the Saxons the area of the South Downs would have been divided into 'hundreds', which served as taxation and administrative units. The hundred, in theory, was supposed to contain 100 'hides', a variable measure of taxable value linked to an area of land. The meeting place of the hundred court to administer justice and regulate local affairs was usually sited on a notable landmark, often a prehistoric monument such as a round barrow. One such example may be the Hundred Moot of Willingdon, on the Downs near Eastbourne. They could also be sited at the centre of an estate or on neutral territory between estates. The frequency with which trade and exchange took place at such meeting places gradually increased their importance as markets. There were about forty such hundreds in Hampshire, including those of East Meon, Selborne and Meonstoke within the South Downs National Park (Walks 13 & 14). Before the Norman Conquest of 1066 the increase in commercial activity, allied to maritime trade and the periodic need for defences, led to meeting places emerging in growing towns or *burhs*, many of them ports, where the minting of coinage had become established. Early towns included the ports of Lewes, Steyning and Arundel, as well as the administrative and ecclesiastical centres of Chichester and Winchester (Walks 2 & 15).

Buying and selling were closely controlled during the Middle Ages, and the Lord of the Manor had to obtain a grant to hold a market in his local town. Grants given were normally for a weekly market and perhaps a three-day annual fair. Trading came under such close scrutiny because the Crown and the local lord could exact taxes and tolls from the movement of goods and their exchange. New meeting places emerged in such markets, characterised by the familiar market square (often they were rectangular or triangular) in surviving towns throughout the South Downs National Park; places such as Alfriston (granted market rights 1406), Findon (1261), Harting (1271), Petersfield (1232), Meonstoke (1247) and Selborne (1270) (Walks 10, 12, 13 & 14). The market at Bishop's Waltham, the site of a palace and town of the Bishop of Winchester, was in existence by 1273 and demonstrates that ecclesiastical as well as lay lords could benefit from taxing trade. Markets often contained market crosses, such as those at Alfriston and Chichester, and market halls, the former to mark the sites where trading could take place and the latter were originally timber-framed buildings, raised on pillars. The open ground floor provided shelter for stall holders in foul weather, especially those selling perishables like butter, while the upper floors were used for administration. A fine example is that from Titchfield, near Fareham, now on display within the Park at the Weald and Downland Museum. Annual fairs on the Downs were often agricultural in nature. Sheep were driven in large flocks to fairs, such as the one at Findon, where an annual three-day fair was in existence as long ago as 1261 and survives to the present.

Market trading was thirsty and tiring work, and every market square was soon surrounded by a number of alehouses and inns – the new meeting places, the pubs of which many of us are so fond! Beer was one of the most common drinks, consumed by all social classes, and it also supplied much of the required daily calorific intake. The public houses provided food, drink, beds, and stables for horses. There are any number of examples scattered throughout the South Downs National Park such as The Bricklayers Arms (Midhurst), The White Hart (Lewes),

The Downs have always been home to special occasions. Beyond the bank of the Iron Age hill fort at the Trundle, the Goodwood Racecourse now provides the venue for those wanting a special day out.

The George (East Meon and also Alfriston), all bearing witness to the innate and enjoyable need for people to meet. During the Industrial Revolution of the eighteenth and nineteenth centuries, brewing was a very important industry, second only to cotton, and before the advent of widespread domestic lighting and reliable water supplies, most sociable activities, and even meetings concerning parish administration, took place in the 'pub'.

If pubs constitute the first stirrings of what has come to be known as the leisure industry then the discovery of the curative powers of sea water provided the frenzy. The later eighteenth century saw the recognition of the supposed medicinal qualities of bathing in the sea, leading to the development of seaside resorts such as Brighton and encouraging great numbers of people from places such as London to cross the Downs by horse and carriage – and from the mid-nineteenth century by train – to reap the benefits of the seaside. The first generations of visitors to the coastline of Hampshire and Sussex probably did not appreciate the quality of the downland landscape, but by the late nineteenth century, tastes had changed, and the quintessential qualities of the area, allied to growing interests in natural history and antiquities, led to the increasing popularity of the Downs. There was, however, a considerable discrepancy between the poverty of some farming downland lives and the comparative wealth of those who could afford to escape the urban grime and enjoy the rural scenery. The historic legacy of this early tourism is still with us today. You can just about make out some of the remains of an early funfair on Devil's Dyke (Walk 4), as well as enjoy horse racing at Goodwood and Brighton, cricket at Petersfield (on a pitch surrounded by prehistoric burial mounds – Walk 12) and polo at Cowdray. More recent activities catered for on the Downs include golf with innumerable courses (e.g., West Meon) and paragliding at Caburn (Lewes) and Old Winchester Hill (East Meon – Walk 13). The most recent manifestation of the need for humans to meet occasionally in larger groups must be the Amex Community Stadium (just outside the South Downs National Park), home to the Seagulls, Brighton and Hove Football Club.

The long and convoluted ancestry of meeting places, from causewayed camps of 6,000 years ago to the Amex Stadium of 2012, is threaded together by the need for human beings to meet, gather, greet and forge relationships in common undertakings. It has always been thus. Another shared and enduring characteristic is the need to believe in powers beyond the everyday. It is those forces that we now want to summon.

BELIEFS, RITUALS AND RELIGIONS

Members of past communities in the South Downs National Park have always felt the need to believe in some external powers in addition to the forces under their immediate and obvious control. The hunter some 8,000 years ago needed to be able to predict where herds of deer might shelter or ensure that a carefully laid fish trap was sufficiently enticing. Early pastoralists and farmers wanted newborn calves to struggle to their feet quickly or the sun to warm the soil, tempting forth green shoots from the seed. The first metallurgists shaping copper then bronze tools, and finally iron implements, sought guarantees that their smithing furnaces would be hot enough to make metal malleable but not brittle. So much in daily lives was unpredictable, so much outside of human control, that help was needed in the form of a body of beliefs and rituals that could tell the future and improve the chances of successful outcomes. Good and bad spirits could live anywhere: on the tops of the Downs, in clearings or in woodlands, in quiet dry valleys, in storm clouds and heat haze, in ponds, rivers and wells, and in pits underground. They could inhabit all manner of live things, from human witches to animals, fish, insects and flowers. They could lurk in useful objects – axes, arrowheads, quern stones, windows and doorways – as benevolent or malevolent forces or capriciously fluctuating between both. And they could be concealed in the unusual. Fossils such as sea urchins are sometimes found on the Downs. Known as shepherds' purses, up to the nineteenth century they were thought to be good luck charms. But the burial of a woman on Whitehawk causewayed camp some 6,000 years ago, complete with a pair of sea urchins, tells us that such things were credited with special powers millennia ago. There were a lot of spirits and they were everywhere – during night and day, when sleep and awake. You could converse with them or curse them, placate or annoy them, but in the long run you needed them on your side to survive.

Surmising from anthropological studies of surviving hunters, the first hunters who lived in the area of the Park no doubt undertook numerous rituals and made plentiful offerings to ensure a successful hunt. They apologised to the trees they felled with their flint axes in order to make woodland clearings. They murmured quiet spells when they laid clumps of ivy in the cleared spaces as fodder for deer. Crouching down in concealed hollows, they called forth the spirits of the deer herd to offer to them one animal that could be sacrificed. When that animal was killed by multiple hunting arrows the hunters were both excited but also grateful for the gift received. Offerings of plants and berries were left behind by way of thanks. It was important that a relationship of goodwill was maintained between hunter and hunted, gatherer and gathered. Hunting wild boar, hooking fish, trapping birds and rodents, and returning to harvest protein and fat-rich hazelnuts were always activities in which a little luck was needed.

From around 4000 BCE a different direction was given to subsistence activities, with more emphasis on pastoralism and agriculture, and a gradual need to identify more closely with certain fixed places in the landscape of the Downs. Some of these were the causewayed camps, noted above, and are represented in Sussex by sites such as the Trundle and Barkhale in the west, and Offham and Combe Hill in the east (Walk 3). At some of these meeting places we can detect the traces left over from a number of rituals. First there is ample evidence for feasting, and feasting usually implies celebration and thanks – witness Thanksgiving Day in the United States and Canada, or its European equivalent, the Harvest Supper. There are also other indicators: a carved bone phallus from the Trundle might be interpreted as a fertility or good-luck token, or something to ward off the evil eye. From the same site, a carved chalk block with a spoke-like decorative pattern could be an attempt to depict the sun, or a feathered cape around the neck of a shaman or other ritual leader. At Offham, near Lewes, a pit contained the smashed fragments of a pottery bowl, a flint leaf-shaped arrowhead and bones from deer, cattle, pig and beaver. The deliberate and violent breaking of any made object is usually a sure sign of something abnormal. There are any number of possible reasons, but if this pottery bowl was used to contain ritual substances, it may have been deemed too dangerous for mortals to reuse, hence its deliberate concealment. A crouched human burial from Offham of a young man found in the ditch of the enclosure is suggestive of another common type of belief: the power of ancestors or witches.

Copper and bronze weapons and tools appeared in the South Downs National Park in slowly increasing numbers from around 2000 BCE. Copper and bronze implements were prized items, manufactured away from settlements using esoteric and seemingly magical expertise, from materials initially won from the earth. Despite how odd it now appears to us, some of these desirable artefacts were surrendered back to the earth, buried in deposits that archaeologists call 'hoards'. Such a term implies safe-keeping and potential later retrieval, but the reality was that some of these hoards were given to be kept safely by the spirits of the underworld forever. Many such hoards were buried on dry ground but often close to rivers, pools and springs, arguing that some kind of water deity might have been revered. Find spots occur from Buriton and Langrish, in the west, to Firle and Iford, in the east. There were a number of metalwork deposits close to the source of the Rother. At Buriton, a palstave (a type of bronze axe) was found on the edge of a steep-sided valley cut into the greensand, close to another spring. There is a cluster of three finds at Langrish, two of which are on sloping ground where water collects at the junction of the chalk and greensand. At Bramber, where the Adur cuts through the chalk, a Late Bronze Age hoard contained ninety-eight items (mostly spearheads), together with human and animal bones, burnt flints, pottery and possible crucible fragments. The deposit had been placed in marshy ground.

In the ensuing Iron Age, the centuries before the Roman Conquest, beliefs and rituals still seem to have involved the breaking, some of which was deliberate, and burial of objects in the ground. Within the hill fort of the Caburn, just east of Lewes, more than 140 pits contained a whole host of different objects, including weapons, iron knives, weaving combs, loom weights, broken quern stones and occasional human jaw bones. Since the Caburn does not seem to have been a permanently settled occupation site, the impression is that people were intermittently climbing up that steep hill, carrying broken or complete artefacts, to bury them at the climactic moment of specific rituals. What were these rituals for and who were they aimed at? Conceivably, there was a vast pantheon of underworld deities honoured through such practices, or perhaps the spirit lay within the artefact itself, the specific comb, knife or weapon. A specimen offered by way of ritual sacrifice may have increased the earthly power of the artefacts that remained. At the Trundle myriad small pieces of broken quern stones were found in pits, too small to be the result of accidental breakage. Do these suggest offerings to a fertility deity, deliberate sacrifices or the intentional burial of a worn-out but respected object that had 'died'?

At the snub end of a stretch of Downs, the hill fort at the Caburn affords extensive views down the river Ouse to the sea.

The southern side of the hill fort bank at the Trundle. The site dominates the West Sussex coastal plain and enjoys views across to the Isle of Wight.

During the Roman period in the area now designated the South Downs National Park there was a concentration of rituals and religion in the first built structures that could be described as 'temples'. Examples occur at Lancing, Slonk Hill (Shoreham), Chanctonbury Ring (Walk 7), Bow Hill (above Chichester) and at Hayling Island, to the south of the Park. However, these are not the classical multi-columned buildings found in the Mediterranean world, but small, square, circular or polygonal buildings that owe much to local conceptions of construction methods and building forms. The gods worshipped in these places were probably a conflation of classical deities and Iron Age gods. Worship is probably the wrong term. The numbers of coins found at some of these sites demonstrates that there was something mercenary about human/divine relationships. You made offerings (i.e. paid) for the intervention of particular gods, and if they proved ineffective, you probably went to another temple. Some of the characteristics and practices at these temples – their siting within Iron Age hill forts and the burial of ox and pig skulls – suggest some continuity of indigenous ritual practice. Rituals and religious beliefs are never uniform in any society; there are always variations of practice and sometimes completely contrary notions of what constitutes proper forms of worship. Lastly, there is more than a hint that some of these 'temples' were the destinations for pilgrimages. Their out-of-the-way but highly visible locations (Hayling Island, Bow Hill, Chanctonbury) strongly suggests that the effort people made in getting to them was part and parcel of their veneration.

The Anglo-Saxons introduced a variety of pagan practices to communities in the Park area, not least in terms of burial rites. Saxon religion drew on its

Germanic homeland and Iron Age traditions. It was polytheistic in character and also revered supernatural entities which inhabited the landscape, such as elves and dragons. Worship took place at regular festivals and involved the sacrifice of inanimate objects and animals. There are hints of such practices at the later Saxon settlement of Bishopstone (Newhaven). Although the elite at Bishopstone were nominally Christian, the remains of animals in pits appear to be from pagan rituals. Christianity eventually spread throughout the Park region, suppressing overt paganism, with the creation of bishoprics at Winchester and Chichester and the establishment of minster churches, the predecessors of later parish churches. For example, minster churches existed at Winchester, Chichester, Singleton, Arundel, Steyning, Lewes and probably Bishopstone. New religious establishments after the Norman Conquest spread the faith further, with multiple foundations of parish churches, monasteries, friaries and priories, many endowed with considerable estates. These are scattered throughout the Park and include such sites as the priories at Southwick, Boxgrove, Lewes (Walk 2) and Wilmington, and abbeys such as Titchfield. At Steyning the Normans respected the area's earlier Christian associations, building their church probably close to the shrine of St Cuthman, which had become a site of pilgrimage in the tenth century.

The legacy of the Church of Rome in and around the new South Downs National Park is an evocative one. Walking around the ruins of once grand priories like that at Boxgrove or visiting quiet parish churches, such as Upwaltham north of Chichester, East Meon, or Clayton, shaded below the chalk escarpment south of Hassocks, it requires an effort to imagine just how central such establishments were to daily lives. Monasteries were some of the wealthiest institutions in medieval society. Peasants were sometimes required to work on ecclesiastical land for no payment and had to give a percentage of their agricultural produce (a tithe) to the Church. In return, the Church provided the only guaranteed way of entering heaven and avoiding purgatory or

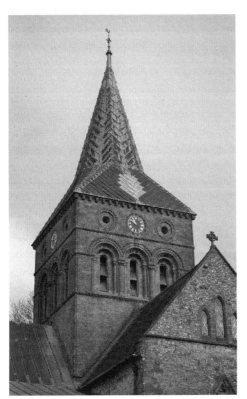

The church of All Saints, East Meon, Hampshire. Probably built between 1080 and 1150. This is an impressive Norman church in a rural setting.

hell. The rich elite of society also were in thrall to the attractions of the after-life, but frequently avoided having to suffer any personal deprivation to get there. Instead they occasionally provided chantries in churches and paid monks to pray for their souls after death.

The break with Roman Catholicism during the English Reformation led to the break-up of the large ecclesiastical estates and the establishment of the Church of England. Parish churches throughout the area of the Park were gradually refurbished in a new Protestant ascetic, one that eschewed the ornate flamboyance of colourful Catholic statuary and wall paintings, and replaced it with more austere fixtures and fittings. The religious persuasion of most people worshipping within our area was Anglican, and in some cases fiercely anti-Catholic, as is remembered in the annual Lewes bonfire celebrations which commemorate, amongst other things, the burning of the Protestant martyrs. Alternative forms of Christian worship, such as those practised by Methodists, Quakers or Baptists, gradually provided some variety in the eighteenth and nineteenth centuries, even more so in Hampshire (Walk 12). The Sussex Methodist churches of Ashington (closed 2010), Steyning and Storrington form a downland trio, while those in Winchester and Fareham are examples of the Baptist movement. The Jireh chapel in Lewes originally housed a Calvinistic congregation (Walk 2). But despite the pervasive influence of various forms of Christianity within the Park, old superstitions still persisted, acted out in tandem with the national religion. The occasional find of a shoe or other object concealed in the chimney of a country cottage, or the burial of a witch bottle, like that from Michelham Priory, is testimony to the enduring fear of the evil eye, and the co-existence of official religion and personal belief.

The modern period, with its rationalism, two world wars, increased social mobility and its emphasis on commercial and technological progress have shredded the former sense of parish cohesion that once bound communities together, in the Park and elsewhere. With a dwindling number of parishioners, some churches and chapels have become less places of worship and more picturesque historical monuments. To the casual visitor, they seem imbued with the religiosity of former times, rather than being epicentres of contemporary religious fervour. New religious establishments in the South Downs National Park – the mosques of Brighton and Winchester, and the Chithurst Buddhist Monastery (Thai Forest Tradition) between Midhurst and Petersfield – speak both of the effects of globalisation and of alternatives to predominantly Western values. As does the continued spirituality of the Long Man of Wilmington. In providing the foci for different beliefs and rituals, they continue a tradition in the Park that began some 6,000 years ago.

Beliefs, rituals, superstitions and religions all promise some sort of individual and communal spiritual protection. But human beings often require more materialistic and tangible signs of being able to safeguard themselves and their kin. It is these more obvious monuments of shelter and security that we visit next.

DEFENSIVE DISPLAYS

While the archaeological and historical evidence from the South Downs National Park provides plentiful confirmation of the need of human beings to believe in things beyond mortal understanding, there is also equally abundant testimony to demonstrate that there were frequent episodes of physical aggression and protection. The first millennia of occupation in the Park – that by hunters and gatherers, the first farmers and metalworkers – have left little trace of defended strongholds. However, the lack of such sites should not persuade us that life was always peaceful. From evidence elsewhere in the country, and from studies of surviving hunters and gatherers in other parts of the world, the propensity for domestic and community violence is always present. Those flint-tipped hunting arrows or wooden-handled stone axes can also inflict serious injury and death. Perhaps the bouts of fighting were shorter, less organised and not sustained, but it is likely that they existed.

Just before the onset of the Iron Age, around 800 BCE, there is evidence of climatic deterioration: there was more rainfall, making some lands too wet to cultivate. This may have significantly waterlogged soils on the coastal plain and in the Weald. Whether this pressure on resources provided an environmental trigger for defensive displays is problematic. However, it is during this period that the first large-scale apparently defensive structures appear in the Park: the hill forts. There are a number of these sites scattered along the Downs, particularly along the impressive north scarp, overlooking the Weald. They stretch from Old Winchester Hill (Walk 13) and St Catherine's Hill (Walk 15) in the west, through Harting Beacon, Chanctonbury (Walk 7), Wolstonbury (Walk 4) and Ditchling Beacon, to Seaford Head and possibly Belle Tout in the east. When you visit them today, you see grass-covered earthen banks, pierced by one or two entrances, encircling turf-covered interiors of varying extent. Don't be lulled by those gently sloping earthen perimeters. In the Iron Age many would have had vertical faces of timber, turf and stone. The hill forts come in all sizes – large (Cissbury), medium-sized (Hollingbury) and small (Caburn) – and all shapes: oval (Wolstonbury) to almost rectangular (Harting Beacon – Walk 10).

Describing hill forts is much easier than explaining what they were for. They do seem to be, in part, related to defence and protection. However, studies have demonstrated that some of the so-called defensive earthworks or 'ramparts' are just too oddly sited to have functioned in that way. The northern perimeter of Devil's Dyke seems too far down a precipitous slope to have worked (Walk 4). Display and defence are frequent bedfellows and in many hill forts an impressive demonstration of power through highly visible barriers may have been more important in making a statement to neighbours than manning them to repel attackers. Excavations within hill forts have clearly indicated that no two are identical: some have evidence for many round-houses and four-post granaries; others for crafts such as metalworking, while some enclose wide and open spaces for the protection of livestock, including much-prized horses. Nor can we be sure who dwelt in them, whether seasonally or all year round. The possible permutations of chiefs, warriors, craft-workers, religious leaders and captive slaves seem as numerous as the hill forts themselves. Daily life, for most people, was acted out in fields and farmsteads outside of hill forts. Whatever the precise range of functions of these impressive hill forts, we need to avoid thinking about them as a sort of prehistoric 'town', occasionally withstanding 'sieges'. Those terms are best left for the medieval period.

Right at the end of the Iron Age, just before southern Britain became an outlying part of the Roman Empire, large-scale earthworks, enclosing vast areas, were constructed north of Chichester (the so-called Chichester Dykes) and in the Winchester area (Oram's Arbour). Again the precise range of activities that took place within these banks is not well understood. However, it is likely that forms of trade and exchange occurred, probably on a periodic basis. You would think that the advent of Roman legions in 43 CE to southern Britain brought the first proper military camps and forts. It did, but not in the area of the South Downs National Park, apart from later posting stations at Milland (near Midhurst) and Hardham (near Pulborough). The reason for this is quite straightforward. This area of the south coast had long enjoyed productive relationships with northern Gaul and when the Romans arrived there were few pockets of resistance south of the Thames and east of the Solent. The result was that daily life continued much as before, especially in rural areas, the only difference being that previous tributes to a local chief now became taxes to a colonial official. It is true that the Roman administration encouraged town life, particularly at Winchester and Chichester.

The white house at Milland sits atop a Roman enclosure. The ditch can be seen to the right of the house, as can the corner of the enclosure. Thought to be a *mansio* or posting station, it may once have accommodated, fed and watered travelling officials and horses on the road from Chichester to Silchester.

Burpham, near Arundel, is one of a series of *burhs* (fortifications) ordered by Alfred the Great or his successor, Edward the Elder, in about 800 CE to defend Sussex from the Vikings. This substantial earthen bank defended a large promontory. The Saxon term *burh* is incorporated into the place name.

How successful these new towns were is debatable. In their first two centuries they did not have masonry town walls, and were small and under-populated. Although Chichester was surrounded by bastioned walls late in the Roman period, this may have been more do to with perceived threats from seaborne invaders, rather than a bold statement of urban prosperity.

If the area of the South Downs National Park is fortunate, situated in the mildest climatic zone of Britain, covered with thin but fertile soils, and flanked by heavier, but equally fertile terrain, it has one obvious weakness, exploited by aggressors on a number of occasions: proximity to the sea, and to the Continent. The Anglo-Saxon Chronicle records the arrival of Aelle and his sons in 477 CE, and his subsequent attack on Anderitum (Pevensey) in 491 CE. Waves of Saxon settlers followed, either living in separate settlements amongst the surviving Romano-British population or occasionally occupying areas by force. The south coast was even in reach of the Vikings for a few centuries. It is only with the Battle of Ellingsdean (West Dean, north of Chichester) in 1001 CE that the Vikings make their historical entrance into the Park area, but the defensive stronghold at Burpham on the Arun, a Saxon fort or *burh*, and the reuse of Roman fortifications at Chichester by King Alfred and his son Edward the Elder, demonstrate that the former sons of Saxon raiders eventually became the fathers of downland defenders. Similar defensive *burhs* were constructed at other locations in or around the Park, including Lewes, Chichester and Winchester. But if the Vikings never managed to settle in the South Downs National Park, their successors – the Normans – certainly did.

THE ARCHAEOLOGY OF THE PARK: THEMES WHILE YOU WALK

The Norman Conquest ushered in the great age of castle building in the South Downs National Park. Castles were a completely novel type of fortification, and permission from the king was needed for their construction. They were much smaller than prehistoric hill forts, Roman towns or Saxon *burhs*, indicating clearly that they were not designed to defend most of the population, but only the new, foreign elite and their families and close associates. The earliest castles, post-1066 CE, are known as 'motte and baileys': essentially earthen mounds topped with timber towers protecting lower courtyards defended by earthworks. Later castles were built in stone. Castles were just not defensive structures and, in fact, few of them suffered regular siege or assault. Rather they were the bases from which offensive actions could be mounted. They also acted as administrative centres for the new lords, to whom pledges of loyalty could be made and various feudal services performed. Motte and bailey castles once existed throughout the Park, such as at Winchester, Rowland's Castle, Chichester, Midhurst, Edburton (Walk 5) and Lewes. The organisation of Sussex was unique in the Norman period, as previously noted. The Downs, and some of the Weald, were divided into six military regions called 'rapes', each one controlled by the castle of a baron. Major masonry castles therefore developed at Arundel, Bramber and Lewes (all in or close to the Park), with easterly fortifications at Pevensey and Hastings.

Norman power was exercised both through military might and divine authority so it is no surprise that there was significant ecclesiastical ownership of lands throughout the Park. Nor is it at all extraordinary that fortifications were constructed for the Church. Wolvesey Castle at Winchester was built for the Bishop of Winchester, Henry of Blois, between 1130 and 1140. When control

Arundel Castle (lower right on the skyline) has been the seat of the Dukes of Norfolk since the eleventh century. The cathedral (top left) was built in the nineteenth century, but in the style of French Gothic of around 1400.

of Normandy was lost in 1204, the English monarchy and prominent lords and ecclesiastics continued to refurbish many castles and religious foundations in stone. At Winchester Henry III added the Great Hall to the earlier Norman fortification between 1222 and 1235 CE. (It now houses a museum of the history of the city.) Increasing tension between France and England from the second half of the thirteenth century onwards saw a wider proliferation of defensive building, including other types of monument. An impressive Barbican Gate was added to Lewes Castle in the 1340s, while grants to construct town walls were given to Chichester (1261), Lewes (1264) and Arundel (1295). The Bishop of Chichester was granted a licence to crenellate a fortified manor house at Amberley, on the Arun, while priories at Michelham and Wilmington were reinforced, the former with an impressive gatehouse and moat. Warblington manor house, in south-east Hampshire, was also moated and fortified around this time.

By 1600 castles had become obsolete, along with the use of the longbow and crossbow. Instead smooth-bore firearms and the use of gunpowder to fire shot were to provide the technological basis for warfare into the twentieth century. Threats, both real and perceived, were still from across, or via, the English Channel, with the French, Spanish and assorted pirates and smugglers the principal culprits. Instead of relying on a collection of feudal lords for defence, the English monarchy, from Henry VIII onwards, began to devise a system of national defence that resulted in a variety of coastal fortifications and gun batteries to repel seaborne attacks. Crucial to the effectiveness of coastal protection was an early warning system and, from the sixteenth century onwards, a number of fire beacons were set up along the length and breadth of the Park to warn authorities of potential threats. Coastal defensive buildings varied in date and design, and included the redoubt at Eastbourne (1804), the chain of Martello towers (taking their name from a tower at Cap Mortella, Corsica, and constructed from Seaford to Aldeburgh in Suffolk) designed to repel a possible invasion by Napoleon, late eighteenth-century brick batteries including two at Brighton, and the Victorian forts at Newhaven and Shoreham. Barracks for troops to defend the coast against the French were built at Exceat (Cuckmere valley) in 1804; some of the foundations and a water trough can still be seen. As the nineteenth century progressed, strategic defence emphasised the increasing role and importance of the Royal Navy, based at Portsmouth, in defending southern Britain from the sea. It was from that port in 1805 that Admiral Nelson sailed for the final time to defeat the Franco-Spanish fleets at Trafalgar, a famous triumph for the nation despite the admiral's tragic death.

The twentieth century, with its two world wars and the ensuing Cold War, has left an indelible historical and archaeological legacy within the South Downs National Park. Some of the great houses were commandeered as centres of military recruitment, and never quite recovered their elitist positions afterwards. The military camp at Hazeley Down, Owslebury, now marked by a commemorative granite cross, was one of the last memories of Blighty for many before they were shipped from Southampton to the muddy chaos of the Somme. Newhaven was a pivotal port from which stores were shipped to the battlefields of northern France. The twice weekly arrivals of wounded from the Front at Brighton station were harrowing spectacles, and the first hospital for shell-shock cases was established in the town. In 1916 Portsmouth experienced its first aerial bombardment from a Zeppelin airship. The Second World War was every bit as intensive in its effect on the Park. A complex of pillboxes, machine-gun posts and anti-tank obstacles were deployed, particularly in the Cuckmere Haven where intelligence suggested a potential German invasion. A rusting Mk II Churchill tank on Kithurst Hill (south of Storrington), left behind by the Fourteenth Canadian Army, is as memorable as it is anomalous (Walk 6). Large manor houses again became home to military personnel, as at Stanmer (Walk 1), while that at Bignor was a centre for the French Resistance. Decoy airfields, with false runway lights, such as that at Gumber, near Slindon, were laid out to fool German bombers. Despite heavy bombing during the war, the docks and beaches of the Solent provided the springboard for the D-Day landings of 1944.

A walker in the South Downs National Park today, admiring the countryside views or visiting some of the celebrated but much earlier heritage, can easily overlook many indications of more recent, twentieth-century military activity. Odd depressions in the turf may mask former slit trenches or foxholes to hide a soldier; brickwork hidden by brambles may signify a pillbox; an incongruous line of concrete may suggest a former anti-aircraft battery. Sometimes this hidden heritage is deliberately deceiving. A slightly isolated but otherwise ordinary-looking bungalow on Truleigh Hill, overlooking the Weald, was designed to be just that – isolated and ordinary – for a good reason (Walk 5). It contained a top-secret intelligence installation during the Cold War. And an underground reservoir at Twyford (near Winchester), only completed in 1990, was designed to protect Southern Water staff tasked with restoring safe water supplies in the event of a nuclear attack. It was an impressive structure, but thankfully never needed.

KEEPING IN TOUCH WITH THE DEAD

At the time of writing Halloween is fast approaching. The dead have always exerted an enduring influence on the living. This is not just in the tricksy event that Halloween has become, but also through the power of mediums, or people who claim to be able to speak to the dead. A topical news story announces that a showstopping celebrity psychic will be offered the chance to demonstrate, in a rigorously controlled setting rather than a theatrical one, that she can really communicate with the dead. A well-known anthropologist, Nigel Barley, also tells a nice story about the ubiquity of ancestors in parts of Africa. He recalls observing a solitary young boy walking along a dirt road, in animated conversation, seemingly with himself. However, the boy claimed he was arguing with some of the ancestors from the village, chastising them for causing an outbreak of illness amongst the living, and urging them to do something about it. The boy was particularly vehement that he had made all the necessary offerings to the ancestors and kept his side of the bargain. (Later, in an admission to the anthropologist, he admits to short-changing the ancestors in some of his offerings.) But the point of this story is that, in many societies, the spirits of the dead are both real and rather ordinary; they are often comforting, sometimes threatening, but likely to cause mischief if ignored. Where can we find the ancestors in the South Downs National Park? In some obvious places, such as church graveyards and war memorials, but also under hundreds of ancient earthen mounds that lie scattered throughout the Park. It's time to meet a few of them.

The very first ancestors are difficult to find. Those early hunters and gatherers in the Park, from around 6,000 BCE, have left no trace of how they cared for their dead. There are no graves or cemeteries, and no locations where human bones or ashes have been discovered. We must assume that they did treat the death of one of their kind as a special event, requiring specific rites and practices. Not all procedures for disposing of the dead would leave permanent marks on the landscape. It is possible that bodies were burnt and ashes scattered on the winds, or that the dead were ceremoniously propped up against a tree by a departing band of hunters and left to dissipate slowly through the forces of nature. As the physical body decayed the tree grew. In such circumstances the tree may even have become the ancestor. But the truth is, for this period, we simply don't know where the ancestors of those early hunters were, and might still be.

With the first farmers in the Park, the ancestors come into sharper focus. We can visit some of their final resting places in a few surviving long and oval earthen mounds. Within the Park they form two small concentrations, one in the east between Brighton and Eastbourne at sites such as Alfriston, Long Burgh and Windover Hill, and one in the west between Chichester and towards Winchester (e.g., Bevis' Thumb, North Marden and Stocks Cottage long barrow – Walk 13). Beyond the Park boundary, close to Andover, lies the excavated site at Nutbane; our most detailed evidence for the ancestors comes from the latter site. The long mound was trapezoidal in shape, wider at the eastern end and flanked by ditches from which the chalk for the mound had been derived. It is clear that the first structural elements, prior to the mound, were a series of timber mortuary houses, containing three crouched adult bodies and one of a child, laid out at different times. After an interval the timber houses were deliberately set on fire, and the whole buried by the construction of the long mound. Remains of broken pottery and animal bones from the eastern or 'forecourt' end suggest that regular feasting probably took place to honour the dead. The oval barrow at Alfriston covered two pits, one of which contained the crouched burial of a young female. The earlier long barrows near Owslebury, and the later oval barrow at Alfriston, must have been prominent landmarks – initially mounds of freshly dug greyish and white chalk. Their construction probably involved many members of the community, who subsequently communicated with the dead by periodically sharing a meal

The roots of a mature tree dig into the remains of a prehistoric long barrow near Owslebury.

with them. These early ancestors may have been the founding pioneers of early farming settlements.

During the millennium of 2500 BCE to 1500 BCE the ancestors multiply considerably in number and their resting places can be identified in the Park by mostly smallish turf-covered round mounds. There must have been thousands of these mounds at one time, with hundreds scattered along the north escarpment of the Downs, with fine views over the Weald, certainly indicating that the dead were meant to enjoy the scenery as much as the living (Walk 6). They also acted, of course, as very obvious territorial markers. The mounds cover a variety of burial forms, including single inhumations and cremations (with the ashes in large ceramic urns) and several separate cremations. Mounds can be standalone or grouped into cemeteries of barrows. Some of the burials beneath the mounds were spectacular. In the 1850s an inhumation in a timber coffin at Hove was accompanied in death by an amber cup, a Scandinavian stone battle axe, a whetstone pendant and a bronze dagger – ably demonstrating that connections by sea always linked the Downs to the Continent. A similar tree-trunk coffin was found in the Great Barrow at Bishop's Waltham. There is a concentration of very large mounds in the Chichester region (e.g., the Devil's Humps at Bow Hill) and along the Rother valley, on the greensand, towards Heyshott Down, Iping Common and Petersfield (Walks 9 & 12). At some of these sites (e.g., the Devil's Jumps near Treyford) there are barrow cemeteries whose long axes point towards the northwest, probably aligned on the midsummer solstice. This suggests that the ancestors lived in ritual landscapes in the Park area, which were more extensive than their individual barrow locations.

If we use our imaginations, we can visualise this ancestral landscape of the Park. Over the 1,000 years of round-barrow burial let's assume that some 4,000 barrows were thrown up. That equates to about four barrows a year. We do not know where these people were living, and it is quite likely that the majority of mourners lived in settlements outside the Park. Nor do we know where the cremation pyres were sited, or even that the majority of the dead received barrow burial. But by, say, 1500 BCE some of the Park must have been so populated by the dead that it resembled one vast cemetery landscape, full of older turf-covered barrows, new whitish chalk barrows, funeral pyres and processions of wailing mourners. All engaged in the very necessary task of keeping in touch with their loved ones. Their ancestors, in return, must have watched over the fields and animals of the living.

Sometimes, however, our imaginations are not good guides to the past. Even some of our imaginings can become constrained by our present-day experiences, the things that we have seen or read about. So although we might imagine 'processions of wailing mourners', this image may be something of a cliché. Knowledge of funeral practices around the world indicates that often such rites can start in a very sombre way, but end up very lively and raucous affairs. Indeed, some claim that the principal point of funerals is to help assuage the grief of the bereaved, so a party atmosphere helps. Our own modern-day wakes are an echo of this tradition. Funerals can be celebrations of a life lived rather than a life lost. Indeed, in 1500 BCE we cannot be certain that 'loss' was felt in the same way that we feel it today. There are thousands of barrows in the Park. But the relationship between the living, standing around them, and their ancestors may have been one of closeness, joy and laughter, as much as sadness.

In the subsequent Iron Age, from 700 BCE, the ancestors, by and large, disappear. There are one or two isolated burials, such as the crouched inhumation from the Goodwood Estate near Chichester, but their rarity suggests there is something abnormal about these. People who die 'bad' deaths, such as those who have died from an accident or as a result of being a witch during life, are often treated as outcasts in death. What became of the dead? One theory is that, as many elaborate weapons of this period are found in rivers, the watercourses and streams of the Park must have swallowed up mortal remains. Some have even suggested that the taboo on fish eating that seems to have been practised by the living was caused by this method of disposal. There are a few exceptions. A flat cremation cemetery at Westhampnett, just east of Chichester, dating from 100 BCE, contained the remains of 161 individuals. The pottery accompanying them, however, suggests that they were recent immigrants from the Continent. At Owslebury, in Hampshire, a man was buried with a shield, sword and spear – a so-called 'warrior burial'; he may have been the much-revered founder of the settlement.

The Romans wanted to control the dead as much as the living. They both respected and feared the ancestors – other people's ancestors as much as their own (Walk 9). Near the Park area one of the largest Roman cemeteries is that at St Pancras outside the east gate of Chichester. The estimated surface area of the cemetery in antiquity was some 2 hectares, and up to 10,000 people could have been buried there between 70 and 250 CE. On average, one person a week, after the cremation rites, would have been interred – a very frequent occurrence which no doubt was noted ominously by most of the inhabitants of the town. Some of the dead, most of them locally born, were accompanied by a variety of jugs and plates from which to eat in the afterlife. There were clearly status distinctions to maintain among the dead. Another early cremation cemetery existed at Alton, while a later urban cemetery of inhumations was excavated at Lankhills, Winchester. Cremation persisted into the early Anglo-Saxon pagan period, and there are a number of early cemeteries between the rivers Ouse and Cuckmere in the east of the Park. At Alfriston the ashes of two of the dead of a small community were placed in distinctive pedestalled pots with bosses on them; however, most were inhumed, males accompanied by a sword, shield or axe, women by elaborate brooches. A potential link with the earlier Romano-British population is also evident at the cemetery at Itchen Abbas, near Winchester, which spans the late Roman to early Anglo-Saxon periods.

With the arrival of Christianity that long age of ancestral veneration was seemingly coming to an end, to be replaced by a much more organised and controlled worship of a supreme god and a tradition of east–west orientated inhumation burials. On a small hill at Apple Down, north-west of Chichester, the excavation of two cemeteries demonstrated this transition. The first cemetery, in use until *c.* 700 CE, contained a mix of cremation and inhumation burials, associated with small timber structures covering cremations that may have been 'houses for the dead' or family shrines visited for generations. The second cemetery, located right on top of the hill, was slightly later and contained nine east-facing inhumations of people who may well have been baptised Christians. Not that all the dead were God-fearing. As a national government emerged and began to tighten its grip on local communities, execution and associated burial sites, like the one on Stockbridge Down in the Test valley, became more common. Here was the grave of someone who had managed to hide a small stash of pennies from his executioners in around 1065. Another had been put in the grave without his head, as had a dog. Polite 1930s interpretation saw this as man and hound punished for illicit hunting; the more explicit 1990s saw it as punishment for bestiality.

Yet the ancestors haven't simply disappeared. Throughout the South Downs National Park one of the most evocative places to feel the presence of the dead is in the graveyards of its hundreds of parish churches (Walk 9), as well as the associations of the dead with religious institutions such as monasteries, priories, friaries, hospitals and, after the Reformation, chapels. There is nothing quite so emotive as wandering among overgrown graves and discoloured headstones in some country graveyard, trying to decipher their symbolism, names, dates and family relationships, and to reflect on the sorrows of widows, sons and daughters. There is a different sense of time in these places, an ancestral atmosphere that threatens to become more tangible the longer you linger. Often you exit gratefully through an old lych gate to breathe more easily in the land of the living.

These two gravestones mark the last resting places of John Heather (left) and Mary, his wife (right), in the cemetery of Bignor parish church. The togetherness of the identical gravestones is a touching memorial.

Sometimes, when former religious establishments have disappeared, your imagination has to work harder. Under arable fields outside Winchester lies the hospital of St Mary Magdalen, where apparently the leprous dead were laid to rest before the Norman Conquest. Over 100 medieval burials were located at the Hospital of St Nicholas in Lewes (Western Road), long since buried itself by urban buildings. Excavations of part of the cemetery revealed bodies buried in shrouds and coffins. Some were more prosperous and may have been buried in drier chalk graves, some unfortunate, buried with manacled legs or arms tied behind their backs, suggestive of execution. Life expectancy was short in the medieval period and cemeteries often filled up quickly, hence the occurrence of charnel pits, where the rested dead were exhumed and reburied en masse. The Hospital of St James and St Mary Magdalene, just outside Chichester, was founded as a leper hospital for men in the twelfth century, surviving the Reformation by becoming an alms-house for the sick poor. Nearly 400 graves were excavated prior to new building on the site. It was a doomed life, however, as a leper. There was no cure and, indeed, if you attempted one you would be thwarting divine will. The benefits came to the carers. If you founded a leper hospital and the inmates prayed for you, your time in purgatory would be lessened.

The twentieth century has also left its reminders of the departed throughout the Park. The innumerable war memorials remembering the dead of the two world wars at places big and small, such as Winchester, Petersfield, Hinton Ampner, Rowland's Castle, Chichester, Lewes and Jevington (Walks 2 & 3), silently record the suffering of some for the survival of others. During the First World War over

The war memorial at Petersfield (Walk 12). The references to more recent wars at the bottom of the listings bring home the local impact of distant conflicts.

800,000 Indian troops fought for the Allied powers. King George V wanted some of the wounded Indians to be cared for at Brighton Pavilion, where he hoped the flamboyant Indo-Saracenic architecture would provide appropriate quarters. The bodies of fifty-three Hindus and Sikhs were taken thence to a location high on the South Downs above Brighton, where a *ghat* (funeral pyre) was built so they could be cremated and their ashes scattered in the English Channel. A small, isolated, tower-like structure, the Chattri – gleaming white Sicilian marble viewed against the brilliant greens and blues of a summer downland morning – now marks the spot where cremation pyres once burned. In even more recent times, the dead within the South Downs National Park, like the dead of those very first hunters, are there but unseen. The practice of scattering human ashes is quietly undertaken by mourners. On bright sunlit days or brooding cloud-covered ones, in places with views that stretch the eye or quietly secret spots, ashes are sprinkled and blown like seed. They are special places for those who want to keep in touch with the ones they loved. They make them live in the present. And that is where they join us in our final story.

THE PAST IN THE PRESENT

When you go for a stroll in the South Downs National Park you travel from one place to another: you walk up a hill or down a high street; you amble along the bottom of a dry valley or along the top of the chalk escarpment, looking out over the great wooded expanse that is the Weald of England, and occasionally glimpsing a triangle of blue behind you that is the English Channel. Your journey is very much in the present. When you return home you expect things to be pretty much as you left them – and they will be. But the beauty of the South Downs National Park lies in its uncanny ability to make you forget about the everyday that you have momentarily left behind. The here and now becomes blurred by the past and future. Alone, lost in thought, you can easily seek this transcendence and solace in the downland views. Even as a couple, sheltering in a thicket of gorse or hawthorn from a sudden squall of rain, rice-paper close, conversation faltered – that slightly unnerving sense of timelessness steals quietly up on you. In those moments you are at one with the generations past who have lived, worked, worshipped, defended and enjoyed the area we now know as the South Downs National Park.

If you trudge up a deeply worn track at the edge of the Downs you can pause and imagine the thirsty cowherd driving cattle up to summer pasture or the impatient shepherd and dog hustling a flock down to the sheep fair. Move aside for the noisy quarrymen, sweat-stained and covered in grey chalk dust, loading horse-drawn wagons with blocks of chalk ready for the kilns. At a dew pond you sense the huddle of animals whose shuffling hoofs have trodden the soil around its perimeter into myriad little water-filled depressions. Over your shoulder, in the growing gloom, you think you hear a shepherd, whistling sharply, penning ewes behind hazel hurdles for the night, turning his overnight shelter away from the wind. Just for a second you think you catch the wind-carried laughter of women returning from the fields. There are even echoes of more distant pasts.

Stop and linger by any of the hundreds of round mounds that punctuate the landscape. Like a grammar of past grief, they huddle in clusters or stand isolated as shrub-covered mounds in the middle of ploughed fields. Pause to commiserate with a downcast family burying the ashes of a loved relative in a pottery urn.

Known as 'The Little Church in a field', the isolated church at Idsworth dedicated to St Hubert is probably Norman in origin. This simple church is renowned for its medieval wall paintings.

Or idle along the grass-covered banks of an Iron Age hill fort and smell the sweet smoke from a pig roast and listen to the noisy laughter of the large gathering within. Walk along the now narrow flinty road known as Stane Street (Walk 8) that once connected Chichester to London, occasionally pausing to listen or move smartly to let a wagon bound for market, laden with sheepskins, pass. From the top of a rise marvel at matchstick men on flimsy wooden scaffolding, hauling blocks of greensand, binding them in to the flinty cobbled corners of a tiny, distant church.

Do not relinquish your time travels just because you reach the High Street (Walks 2 & 12). Despite the bustle, your imagined journey is easier here. You can strip the centuries from the building façades that confront you, like layers of an onion. The elegant Regency or Georgian exteriors are passed by horse-drawn carriages with passengers destined for a night at the local coaching inn. Behind these frontages lie timber-framed medieval town houses, each room occupied by a different family, some preparing goods for the weekly market. Earlier still are the great castles, priories and friaries, full of people bent on taking your labour in this world and saving your soul in the next – your life and afterlife are simply not your own. The few streets are murky thoroughfares – you hang on to your coins in case a cutpurse is about, and hold your nose as a cart full of cess spills and splashes shakily past on its way to the town's ditch.

Just as we can experience the past of the South Downs National Park, so too did other generations who came before us. They each had their own pasts to contend with. Those first farmers who ventured up on to the Downs *c.* 4000 BCE came across deserted woodland clearings and smouldering camp hearths of hunters who had seen and heard them coming from afar. Communities burying their dead *c.* 2000 BCE often chose to give them a last resting place under mounds close to the causewayed camps of the earlier farmers, as at Barkhale or Combe Hill (Walk 3), while the builders of Iron Age hill forts, in turn, often enclosed and respected the dead of

The Norfolk Arms in Arundel, with its Georgian geometric array of windows and central arch for horse-drawn coaches, must have been a welcome sight for weary and thirsty travellers – and for the horses too. Warmth, ale, food, straw and stabling awaited.

earlier generations, leaving burial mounds intact within their encircling banks, as at Old Winchester Hill (Walk 13). In the Roman period worshippers erected shrines within old hill forts such as Chanctonbury (Walk 7), while the Saxons often buried their dead in earlier prehistoric barrows. The Normans, brash and organised in life, still ensured that they anchored themselves in local religious traditions, building on the fame of local saints, as at Steyning.

The past is, and was, a potent force, to be reckoned and dealt with, often respected, sometimes destroyed, occasionally recreated, but never ignored. Henry VIII knew this well. His agents tore down religious establishments, like Boxgrove, Lewes (Walk 2) and Wilmington priories, throughout the Park. Whole parish churches were stripped of their rood screens, vestments and relics, and statuary was defaced and decapitated, to symbolise the essential purity of the new Church of England. Recalcitrant monks were unceremoniously de-robed. Sometimes a decisive break with the past was required. And sometimes a deliberate link was sought. The parish church at Iping, on the Sussex/Hampshire border (Walk 9), was rebuilt in the nineteenth century, but purposefully in thirteenth-century style. More idiosyncratically, the Gothic and castellated façade of Clayton Tunnel, leading trains under the Downs to Brighton, was finished off with Caen stone, which was surely a nod to those distant Norman castle builders.

The past is in the present in two other major ways within the South Downs National Park. Most obviously, you can see objects from the past in some of the Park's major museums. Many of these items have been excavated or found by chance in the Park during the last couple of centuries, and many of them are quite extraordinary. Inside Barbican House Museum, next to Lewes Castle, are some of the exquisite brooches and other personal adornments, such as beads, rings and tweezers, found with some of the Anglo-Saxon dead at Alfriston. In Hove Museum you can marvel at the amber cup found in a chiefly burial, made from Baltic amber and over 3,500 years old. The translucent qualities of this exotic object demonstrate that even then the desire for something magical, extravagant and rare was beguiling. At Worthing Museum you can see at first hand some of the products from the earliest flint mines at Cissbury and Harrow Hill, as well as an exceptional fifth-century Egyptian goblet from an Anglo-Saxon cemetery at Highdown. In the museum at Petersfield you can glimpse artefacts from the more recent and local past of the town and surrounding countryside, including the paintings of local town life by artist Flora Twort (1893–1985). In the nearby Rams Walk shopping mall a rather lost shepherd recalls the past importance of sheep to the town (Walk 12). Winchester boasts a number of museums: the City Museum concentrates on the Roman and medieval phases of the modern city, while if you fancy yourself in armour, then the Westgate Museum is the place not only to be seen but also feared.

Museums certainly help to bring some of the minutiae of past lives in the Park back to life. Yet their resurrection is never quite complete. The glass cases that enclose most of the objects are an obvious and necessary evil, but they prevent the

The grand entrance to Clayton Tunnel, which took the railway from Hassocks to Brighton. The entrance was built in 1841. The tunnel keeper's cottage was added in around 1850. The whole Gothic effect draws its inspiration from a much earlier age.

visitor interacting enquiringly with the displayed items – as in, just how much does that sword weigh or what does that collar really feel like? You can only enquire through your eyes, and while they are clearly better than nothing, they can only provide literally and metaphorically one sense of the past. A better appreciation of past lives can sometimes be obtained where museums are constructed around ancient (or replica) buildings – at least you know that the objects in some of the cases have not moved very far from where they were found! Sites such as Butser Ancient Farm (Petersfield) and the Weald and Downland Museum (Singleton) provide imaginative three-dimensional engagements with the past, despite the fact that the buildings are replicas at the former and have been brought from other locations at the latter. And the brand-new museum in Chichester (Novium) invites you to feel the heat from a suite of steamy Roman baths.

The final way the past is present in the Park is a little more subtle but no less real. L.P. Hartley's novel, *The Go-Between* (1953), began with the famous line: 'The past is a foreign country: they do things differently there.' And, of course, in reading this small book, you might well imagine that applies pretty much to past lives in the South Downs National Park. It does, but only to a certain extent. Born in an age where technological changes seem to accelerate year on year, and where, in the not-so-distant but seemingly bleaker and alien world of the 1950s, even most of the people looked grey and thinner, it's easy to think of that inevitable march of time as straight, true and utterly transformative. However, in the past there have been rapid periods of change too: the Reformation and the destruction of monasteries must have been both quick and brutal, while the Industrial Revolution rapidly altered both towns and countryside. And the past is always inescapably in the present, as indicated above. It's also written into our very genes, through repeating cycles of involvement with our environment.

What are those things in the South Downs National Park that repeat, that came, and come, around again? Well, first there were (and are) the seasons of the year – colder in winter, glowing in summer, damper and danker in autumn and invigoratingly fresh in spring. Although moderated by climate change over the millennia, these were much more noticeable to practically every previous genera-tion in the area now designated by the Park. They dictated when animals could be trapped or crops sown. They governed the movements of herds and flocks on and off the Downs. Most significantly, they laid down what you could and could not eat at various times of the year. Hazelnuts, so important a food resource for early hunters and gatherers, were only collected in recent centuries after the feast of St Philbert (22 August), hence their colloquial name 'filberts'. Then there were (and are) the cycles of sun and moon, which were vital to all sorts of prehis-toric and historic beliefs. In the fourteenth century the small-town physician in Midhurst or Lewes was likely to treat your affliction by first enquiring when your illness took hold, since he needed to work out where the sun and moon were at the time to prepare the appropriate concoction. Then there were weekly cycles, in the medieval period consisting of days to work on the lord's manor, days to pray, days to trade at market and days to feast or fast. Finally, there were (and are) cycles of generations – of births and deaths, marriages and estrangements, foreign jour-neys and strange smells, home hearths and familiar beds, war and peace.

It is through these differently geared cycles that lives in the past in the South Downs National Park can be understood, certainly different in degree from our own but not in kind. For some 8,000 years or so people who dwelt in the Park needed to utilise and manage its resources. They had food to find and farm – hunt-ing, trapping, gathering, planting, harvesting and herding. They needed buildings to live in, and places to congregate, socialise, feast, joke and love. At times they had to defend their livelihoods from threats, both near and far. More often than not they clung to supernatural beliefs which would bring them good fortune or pro-tect them from harm. And, when breath itself had failed, they created monuments for the afterlives for the dead and invented traditions to ease the pain of passing and the grief of those left behind. And we, too, do all these things. Not really so much time's straight arrow, then, but time's continuous spiral, shifting in circles but ultimately repetitive – linking the past with the present, and with the future. The past might appear superficially to be a distinctive, foreign country, but lived experiences of ordinary lives provide innumerable elements of continuity. These stories are ultimately both foreign and familiar. So let's begin, let's start walking …

THE WALKS

WALK 1: FEBRUARY

STANMER PARK AND HOLLINGBURY HILL FORT – THE EDGE OF BRIGHTON

IN A NUTSHELL

As you might expect, a walk on the edge of the cosmopolitan city of Brighton is not a particularly quiet one. But the weather is dishwater dull with no prospect of improvement, so we will start somewhere close to home. If you long for the relative tranquillity of countryside, don't worry – there are plenty of treats in store in the other walks. There is a bonus with this one, however, in that much of the land is open access, so you don't necessarily have to stick to the footpaths. There certainly is enough history to keep us busy: burial mounds over 3,000 years old, a pre-Roman hill fort and a great country estate, complete with its Georgian house, church and village. But they are bordered by post-war housing, truncated by the deep valley of the A27 and flanked by the University of Sussex to the east. If you can accept these as part and parcel of the historic landscape then let's walk on and meet the past.

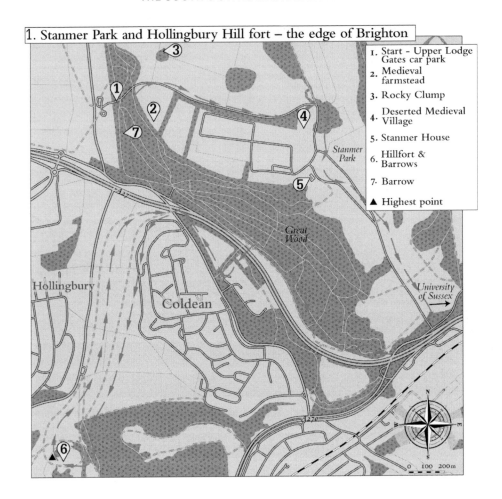

1. Stanmer Park and Hollingbury Hill fort – the edge of Brighton

1. Start - Upper Lodge Gates car park
2. Medieval farmstead
3. Rocky Clump
4. Deserted Medieval Village
5. Stanmer House
6. Hillfort & Barrows
7. Barrow
▲ Highest point

TIME TO GET GOING

Make a start at the small car park to the east of the Ditchling Road (TQ 3239 0989). Walking eastwards, we meet our first buildings. Their purpose is really given away by their number and similarity – there are two of them and they flank a small road that runs between them. They are whitewashed now but were once the eighteenth-century upper lodge gates to Stanmer Park, one of the many private estates in the South Downs National Park. Having two of them appealed to the Georgian sense of symmetry. They housed the gatekeepers to the estate, who could monitor who entered and exited. Even now, walking between them, it's hard not to feel someone unseen is looking at you. Past the lodges, and a small road sweeps northwards and downwards, a wood and coppiced hedge to the north, and there are modern nurseries screened by trees to the south. This is the departing route that must have been used by coach and horses intent on carrying their passengers northwards, across the Downs, descending to Ditchling and the wooded clay lands of the Weald. But this particular estate landscape is much more ancient. Immediately emerging from the wood, in the field to the south are the earthworks of a thirteenth-century farm, lying roughly at TQ 327 098 where the ground flattens slightly. On the other side, a little farther on, in front of the copse of trees, lies a Roman farmstead now known as Rocky Clump (Upper Lodge Wood on the OS map – TQ 327 100). Overlying it was a Saxon cemetery. People have lived and farmed here for millennia.

Reaching the bottom of the incline, and turning right, you are in for a surprise. The principal components of an estate village are laid out before you – houses, a dew pond, a barn, cow stalls and beyond a flint church – nestling almost quietly in a dry valley bottom, half hidden and mostly bypassed by the modern world. Here is a quintessential historic village, whose current form owes much to the Pelham family who succeeded to the estate in 1712. But a village has probably stood hereabouts for the last 1,000 years, its inhabitants owing their livelihoods, and paying their tithes, to great land-owning ecclesiastical or secular lords. Domesday records suggest a thriving community of about thirty families resided here, and a survey of 1608 indicates that the population numbers had changed little. However, the earlier village lay to the west of the current main street. House platforms of the medieval village can be seen in the paddock opposite the tearooms, at TQ 335 097. (Note that there is no access to the paddock, but leaning on the gate will give you

These sarsen stones lie within the copse of beech trees at Rocky Clump. Such sarsens, deposited naturally by geological processes, were once much more widely scattered on the Downs.

Horses now graze over the house platforms and gardens of the medieval village of Stanmer. In the background lie the barn and the church with its spire.

a good view and a bit of a breather.) The landowners who moved the village from its old location to its present position were the Michelbornes, high-minded 'agricultural improvers' fired with the puritanical zeal of the mid-1600s.

We liked the little clutch of tall-chimneyed houses on either side of the village street – walls made of angular flint, and corners and window surrounds of brick. One gable end was fitted out with some white-painted woodwork that seemed to be a nod to the timber-frame building techniques of centuries past. Next to them is a line of cow stalls, running away from the street. When we passed, on this gloomy February morning, a cow and calf were lying quietly under cover, while out in the muddy yard their colleagues jostled and bellowed for fresh hay. The long barn is painted in an unusual soft lime green, with white shuttered doors and windows. Despite its appearance of being something of a period piece, there are facilities for the modern visitor – tearooms, toilets and even a red-painted telephone kiosk. But even these hint at a kind of bygone age of more homely tourism.

Dominating the village, architecturally and spiritually, the spire-topped, slate-roofed, flint-walled church stands at its southern end. In the medieval period every single person in the village would have frequented the church regularly, listening to readings that preached the fear of hell and God's promise of redemption, attending life-cycle moments such as baptisms and confirmations, and offering their tithes for the benefit of the priest. It is hard to imagine just how central and all-pervasive the village church was. Yet the current church, although medieval-looking, is not medieval in date, but nineteenth century, constructed on the site of an earlier church at the behest of the owners of the estate. Like many rebuilt churches in the nineteenth century, the architects designed them in a Gothic revival style, in this case imitating ecclesiastical architecture of the thirteenth century. There are memorials in the graveyard to the Pelham family, who acquired the estate in 1712. Religious fervour faltered during the twentieth century and Stanmer church was deemed redundant in 2008.

Continuing southwards past the church, our walk brings us to the grand north-east façade of Stanmer House. It was designed by a trendy French architect, Nicholas Dubois, in 1722 for the then residents, the Pelhams, incorporating the remains of an earlier house. The house is Palladian in style, drawing its inspiration from the Venetian architect Andrea Palladio, who valued the classical heritage of Italy and the symmetrical proportions of some Roman buildings. Dubois planned a range of rooms around a rectangular courtyard. The front of Stanmer House, with its protruding pediment and dwarf Doric columns surrounding its entrance porch, evokes the great classical temples of Rome, while the geometric arrangement of sashed windows is characteristic of the Georgian love of order.

Like so many other country estates, the two world wars of the twentieth century took their toll on the financial and social supports for elite lifestyles. The War Office requisitioned Stanmer House for the war effort in 1942, and inheritance tax reduced the Pelhams' faltering fortunes still further. In 1946 Stanmer House was bought by Brighton Corporation, although even a shot of public finance failed to curb its decline. In 2004 it was acquired by private investors who

The geometric façade of Stanmer House, with its classical pedimented entrance. It is now a place for fine dining and marriages.

transformed it into the fine-dining and wedding venue it is today. The fates of these two buildings, Stanmer church and house, mirror the transformational effect of the momentous events of the twentieth century on British society. The loss of empire, two world wars and the forces of globalisation weakened national religiosity and brought an end to the domination of the landed classes. In the twenty-first century happy couples are married in Stanmer House while the church by its side is usually locked, silent and empty.

Leaving Stanmer House behind, walk down the main driveway of the house towards the lower lodge gates. Stanmer wood lies to the west, fringing the parkland, on the edge of which stands a commemorative urn on a triangular pillar – a memorial to Thomas Pelham's father-in-law. The complex of the University of Sussex lies just over the horizon to the east. All great country houses were furnished with landscaped parks, and Stanmer is no exception. In the eigtheenth century it must have been a really pleasant ride or walk, once beyond the lower lodge gates, across downland or along quiet lanes, descending to the seaside town then known as Brighthelmstone. And even more beneficial when Dr Russell of Lewes declared that seawater was an efficacious remedy for all sorts of ailments, including scurvy, King's Evil, leprosy, jaundice and glandular consumption. The nineteenth century brought rapid change, however, as the railways carried day-trippers to Brighton, and indeed rail tracks were laid within a few hundred metres of the lower lodge gates.

Turn westwards before you reach the lodge gates and gradually ascend through the woodland paths in the Great Wood of Stanmer. There are multiple paths here so you need to follow the terrain with a sense of direction. Woods once filled with songbird now reverberate to the roar of traffic on the A27 to the south. The trees are mostly beech, but modern management practices have felled most of the older trees and replaced them with younger, straight-trunked specimens. Somewhere hereabouts the scariest archaeological photograph I have ever seen was taken. After a storm in the 1960s, a large beech tree fell, its roots suddenly vertical. In amongst the roots was a virtually intact Saxon skeleton, pulled up from his grave, uprightly transfixed, and feeling fresh air for the first time, after some 1,200 years!

Move closer towards the noise and you come up sharp against the edge of the deep cutting that carries the main road. This was once a gentle downland slope to the south but has now been scarred in the most irrevocable way. On the near horizon, to the south-west, is another elevated section of downland at Hollingbury. That is where we are heading, but the first task is to safely make our crossing. You need to find the northern-most footbridge crossing (there are two bridges), which will take you over the A27. It is located approximately at TQ 333 092. We congratulated ourselves on finding the right footbridge, then imagined ourselves as courageous Andean explorers swaying across one of those rope bridges that span chasms beneath, only they gazed down on foaming rapids while we waved at much faster commuters. Once across, turn sharply right, skirting a small field, then through bordering trees to arrive at the edge of Coldean Lane. Cross carefully, and then go a little way down Saunders Hill, until you can go negotiate the kissing gate on the right-hand side. You have entered the pleasant Hollingbury Park – well done. Now head up the hill and then south for the dew pond, and beyond to the earthwork-surrounded summit.

The summit is crowned by an almost rectangular earthwork, an Iron Age hill fort, from which extensive views of the English Channel and Brighton can be enjoyed. But the hill fort is not the earliest monument. Within the confines of the earthen banks are the remains of four burial mounds that must date to *c.* 1500 BCE. In addition, in 1825 a labourer digging for flint came upon an astonishing find: a hoard of four bronze arm rings, a broken torque (neck ring), three spiral finger rings and a deliberately broken bronze axe head. These finds may well have been grave goods, or a votive deposition, accompanying the cremated remains of the individuals laid to rest in such a spectacular location. A thousand years later, the bank surrounding the hill fort was constructed. Once vertically faced with timber, it enclosed the remains of a few circular round-houses in its more sheltered south-west quadrant. This is Brighton's hill fort and it is hard not to believe that the fort provided a range of communal services for farmers who cultivated the surrounding hills and dry valleys. The Iron Age warriors who may have once whirled sling stones at Hollingbury have now been replaced by equally competitive golfers, who strike their balls with no less effort. Retrace your steps back through the kissing gate, turning northwards up Coldean Lane, under the A27 (path on the left – but note the abutting nineteenth-century estate wall on the right) until you come to an entrance in the flint wall, on the north side of the road. Be careful of the traffic! This flint estate wall was allegedly built by Napoleonic prisoners of war. They seem to have done a good job. Go through the entrance, up to a car park known as the Chalk Pit or Hill, safely back in Stanmer Wood.

The last leg of our walk takes us around the south-western edge of the wood – Old Boat Corner on the map, but in reality there are no suggestions of maritime activity. Make sure you don't cut the corner; there are again multiple choices of paths. Occasionally there are intriguing signs of very recent occupation: a metal cooking pan hooked on tree trunk or a glove jokingly slipped on the end of a branch, by a path, to point the way or make a greeting, perhaps? We spy a young couple in the woods, seemingly camping, a fire lit and an incongruous blue and white umbrella nearby. They ignore us and we hesitate over them, intrigued but not wanting to approach. The lifestyle gap seems potentially too large. Strange to experience this unrequited curiosity in the twenty-first century. We continue onwards a little sheepishly. Further on there are sculptures made from sections of tree trunk – a very solid-looking seat and an imperious throne, with S-shaped carvings on its side. We take photographs of each other posing on them, hurriedly because the wood is wet.

And then suddenly, reminders once again of past lives. Just off the path, to the east, lies an unmistakeable low round mound, another barrow of the same date as those at Hollingbury. What prominent individual lies beneath? This barrow was

The low, prehistoric burial mound in Stanmer Wood. You may just be able to make out the tell-tale depression made by early investigators at its centre.

constructed in the open, a long time before the wood was established, for the mound was originally made from freshly dug chalk and in the year of burial must have gleamed white and shining against a green-grassed background, visible from Hollingbury and a good deal further away. Mournful bereaved or maybe relatives eager and excited to talk to an ancestor must have walked these same paths over 3,000 years ago. But the dead have been disturbed. The mound has a large depression at its centre, a tell-tale sign that in the last few hundred years someone has been looking for treasure: perhaps curious gentlemen from Stanmer House, their ladies idly looking on as labourers toiled on a hot Sunday afternoon; perhaps a poor peasant, at night, by flickering oil lamp, hoping his luck would at last change.

Before we leave the woods, a last backwards glance alights upon a majestic line of mature beech planted either side of a track, no doubt a remnant of landscaped rides for the gentry of Stanmer House and the guests of the Pelham family. A little walk, crushing beech mast underfoot, leads us to the broken and gapped flint boundary wall of the estate that once separated, physically and socially, those within from those without. Emerging from the woods by the upper lodge gates, the sky is still leaden, the weather unchanged and still chilly. But we are not the same.

SOFA STATS

The starting point for this walk is the small car park east of the Ditchling Road and just north of the A27 (TQ 3239 0989). The total length of walk is approximately 10km (6 miles). The elevation range is from 53m to 174m above sea level. Minimum walking time is two hours thirty minutes.

ONE BOOK TO LOOK AT BEFORE YOU GO

Goodfield, J. & Robinson, P. (2007), *Stanmer & the Pelham Family*. Brighton: BN1 Publishing.

WALK 2: MARCH

LEWES TOWN – IN THE FOOTSTEPS OF WILLIAM AND GUNDRADA

IN A NUTSHELL

If there is only one urban walk you must undertake within the boundaries of the South Downs National Park, it has to be a ramble around the historic centre of the town of Lewes. On a bright March morning with the sun playing on buildings of red and grey brick, white stucco, orange-tiled roofs and the chequerboard patterns of flint and stone, the townscape is dazzling on the eye, offering so many intriguing perspectives that the viewer is spoilt for choice. And there is a history behind all these buildings, not just of their age, style and construction, but of their varied occupants – some who made history and most of them who didn't. Despite the wealth of vernacular architecture, and notwithstanding over a millennium of history, the walk is one of up, down and around. For Lewes was founded on a chalk downland promontory overlooking the river Ouse, and the tell-tale ridge tops, slopes and curves of the South Downs can be sensed through the soles of your feet.

TIME TO GET GOING

It makes sense to start our walk at Lewes Castle, high on the High Street and the most prominent historic monument in the town. The first castle was built as a result of the Norman Conquest of 1066. Lands, including Lewes, were given by William the Conqueror to one William de Warenne, who hailed from Varenne in Normandy, and his wife Gundrada. They initially erected a timber fortification on top of a chalk mound (possibly on top of Brack Mount where we will end our walk), but that was soon followed by a masonry structure, partly constructed from Caen stone. If William and Gundrada came back to visit the castle today, however,

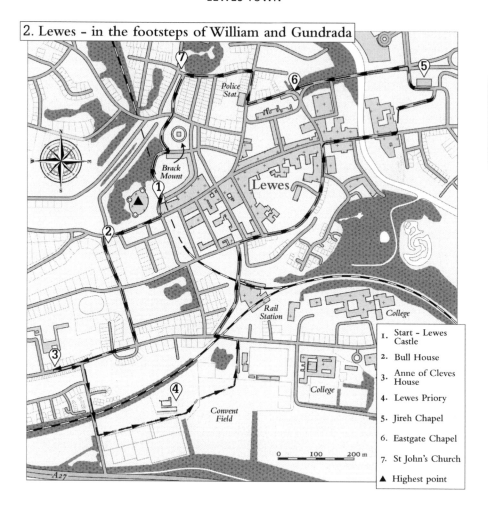

2. Lewes - in the footsteps of William and Gundrada

1.	Start - Lewes Castle
2.	Bull House
3.	Anne of Cleves House
4.	Lewes Priory
5.	Jireh Chapel
6.	Eastgate Chapel
7.	St John's Church
▲	Highest point

they would be pretty confused. They would not recognise the machicolated gateway that stands in front of the Norman one, and they would be quite aghast at having to walk up the attractive zigzagging steps to the keep on top of the mound. The layout of the castle and its bailey (or courtyard) have changed considerably and even they might find the explanatory model just inside the wrought-iron gates helpful in reminding them what it was once like. Adjacent to the castle is Barbican House Museum, a building brick-fronted in Georgian fashion, housing collections relating to Sussex and Lewes.

Norman castles often provided the stimulus for Norman towns, and Lewes was no exception. Out in the High Street façades of different ages compete for street-frontage space. Some are timber-framed buildings that date back to the medieval period, but most were encased by later materials such as brick, tiles, slate and stucco. There are some new builds. A particularly striking example of the latter is the tiled frontage of Bartholomew House, opposite Barbican House. Here the

The Barbican Gate of Lewes Castle. The apertures at the top of the masonry are called machicolations and were for pouring burning oils down on any attackers.

owners, at the start of the nineteenth century, decided to imitate brick facing by simply cladding the building with black, glazed, mathematical tiles. Moving westwards along the High Street, the brilliant white façade of the property in which Gideon Mantell once lived stands out. Mantell was famously the discoverer of the iguanodon, in the Weald of Sussex, and his house, dating from about 1812, fittingly has pilasters topped with representations of ammonites. Further along on the same side is the church of St Michael. Distinguished by its slender spire arising from a round flint tower, its foundation date is not known, but by the time of the Reformation it was in a deplorable condition, materially and spiritually. The round tower is unusual (there are only two others in Sussex, both close by in the Ouse valley) and reputedly its circularity is a product of the difficulty of making quoins (right-angled corners) from flint.

One of the famous parishioners of St Michael's in the eighteenth century was Thomas Paine, author of *The Rights of Man* and *The Age of Reason*. He was married in the church in 1771 to his second wife, Elizabeth Olive. Thomas and Elizabeth lived opposite in Bull House, a timber-framed building dating from the late medieval period. Paine's time in Lewes was a lively one, but not ultimately successful. His radicalism got him dismissed from his position as an excise officer, his marriage failed and his business interests foundered. In September 1774, Paine boarded the *London Packet*, bound for Philadelphia and a political destiny forever linked to the independence of the United States. Just a few more steps, past the site of the West Gate of the medieval town, is a remarkable second-hand bookshop spilling out of a timber-framed medieval building. Books even cling to its external walls for the town's citizens to browse – Tom Paine would have approved, we think.

Time to leave the High Street, turning southwards, to amble down Keere Street (the street of locksmiths) dating from the thirteenth century and built partly over the filled-in ditch surrounding the town. A pebble-flint-filled drain runs down its centre – it must have smelt considerably before the advent of modern drainage. Be thankful you are walking down and not up Keere Street. In the nineteenth

The bookshop at the top of Keere Street in Lewes. Tom Paine would have praised this very public show of literacy.

century the Prince Regent, who had a palace in Brighton, drove a coach and four down this treacherously steep and narrow lane for a wager. You can take your time, admiring the local domestic architectural styles of its terraced houses, particularly the tile cladding and the interplay of grey and red brick on some façades. Continue on at the end of Keere Street, passing Southover Grange – now used as a nursery school and as a location for weddings and exhibitions, but originally built in the sixteenth century of Caen limestone sourced from the demolition of Lewes Priory. The Winterbourne stream runs west to east through its gardens. Make the gentle ascent on the other side of the stream, passing the hospital of St James, founded in the twelfth century, and, resisting the evident charms of the King's Head pub on the corner, turn west along Southover High Street.

First admire, on your left, something architecturally a little pretentiously polite for this market town – an elegant Georgian crescent. Priory Crescent is an unusual (for Lewes) example of a purpose-built, 'polite' terrace of prestigious houses, begun in 1835. Painted stucco and other classical details of the late Georgian period make it both incongruous and attractive. Further west, on the left, rises the brick square tower, topped by a weathervane said to represent a basking shark, of St John the Baptist church. Originally built as a guest house to serve the nearby Priory of St Pancras, the building had become a church by the fourteenth century. The church houses the lead caskets that contained the remains of William and Gundrada, the founders of the priory, whose graves were disturbed by the construction of the Lewes to Brighton railway cutting. It is reasonable to assume that William and Gundrada would not be at all amused by the way history has treated both their gifts to the town, and indeed, themselves.

Our last stop on Southover High Street brings us to the museum known as Anne of Cleve's House. Anne was famous as the fourth wife of Henry VIII and infamous for being compared to a Flanders mare. (Holbein got the blame for painting her too literally: Flanders mares were warhorses – big and strong – and not the dainty fillies fit for queens.) Her marriage to Henry was never consummated but she received a generous divorce settlement, which included this particular building. What she thought of it we will never know, since she does not seem to have visited it. The house is a fifteenth-century Wealden Hall house (but probably with even earlier origins), with a central hearth and hall open to the ceiling. Despite its prosperous origins and brush with the royalty, by the nineteenth century it had fallen on hard times and was in multi-occupancy. Census returns indicate that as many as thirty individuals lived in the house, including a widowed needlewoman and her five children, two spinster sisters, a labourer with six children and a widowed cowkeeper, complete with labourer son and servant daughter.

Leaving Southover High Street by means of Cockshut Road, we walk down and a little ominously under the railway bridge to locate a modest opening in the wall that leads to the site of one of the most grandiose medieval establishments in Norman England: Lewes Priory. The church of the priory and its associated buildings used to tower over this part of Lewes, but sadly have now been reduced

WALK 2

The Prospect Mound next to Lewes Priory. It was a place in the seventeenth century to see from and now functions also as a place to be seen.

to unadorned, but still massive, masonry ruins. Fate was not kind to the priory, and it suffered destruction during the time of the Reformation and when the railway cutting was excavated through what remained of the church. The priory was founded between 1078 and 1082 by William and Gundrada, and was the first Cluniac priory in England (from Cluny, in Burgundy, France). One of the largest surviving structural elements is a toilet block dating from the twelfth century. The cubicles (at least fifty-nine of them) were along the south wall, at first-floor level, with a running sewer at ground level to take away the waste. It takes quite a feat of the imagination to reconstruct the magnificence (and the smells) of this particular priory, but a series of information boards on site with reconstruction drawings certainly help.

In the south-east corner of the priory grounds there is a sculpture of a medieval helmet, erected in 1964 to commemorate the 700th anniversary of the Battle of Lewes. As battles go, this particular one does not get its fair share of publicity. The battle that took place near Lewes in 1264 between Henry III and Simon de Montfort was a pivotal encounter that eventually led to the barons (then headed by Simon) placing restrictions on the autonomy of the monarch. In essence, the long political process that was to lead to parliamentary democracy began in Lewes. The king's army camped at the priory both before and after the crucial engagement. Just to the east of the priory is a large but pleasant grassed mound, known as the Mount, whose summit you can climb. From the top, enjoy a fine view westwards across the remains of the priory and on to the South Downs. The precise origins of this mound are uncertain, but many assume it was built in the seven-teenth century as a garden feature or prospect mound.

It is time to re-join Priory Street and walk past the hustle and bustle of Lewes station before turning right into Lansdown Place. There is a fine terrace of early nineteenth-century houses on the north side of the street – sash windows and arched doorways (complete with black boot scrapes) surrounded by red brick, con-trasting with the smooth façades comprising grey brick headers. The short faces of the bricks allows the creation of a curved corner at the junction of St Nicholas Lane, so rounded and vertical you want to go up and feel its smoothness. They were probably fashioned at the behest of Improvement Commissioners (the fore-runners of local government in England) to ease the safe passage of carts around corners. But they do have an appealing aesthetic. Self-consciousness prevails over tactile curiosity and we move on. On the left are two important ecclesiastical buildings, first of which is the church of All Saints, now the All Saints Centre, which probably dates back to the twelfth century. At the end of the eighteenth century the church was so unsafe that divine service could not be performed within its walls. In a town oversupplied with churches, it eventually failed – hence its current community use. A few paces forward still and you can glance through the railings at the Friends Meeting House (for the Quakers) of 1784, its severe classical porch and brick walling contrasting with the flint tower of All Saints. Actually, the red-brick walling is only real brick for the first metre above ground; above that and around the windows, red and black mathematical tiles were hung on timbers. Take time to explore the area to the north of these buildings, especially the narrow lanes or 'twittens'. These thoroughfares may date back to the Saxon period when the town was a *burh*. Recent excavations here have revealed Saxon features and slight evidence for even earlier activity in the Roman period.

Find your way back to one of the central junctions of the modern town, the bottom of School Hill. Here the traffic lights control and separate the ebb and flow of townsfolk, visitors and the inevitable parade of cars and vans. On the south side of the junction, on the corner, is a small but impressive Gothic revival building – a memorial library constructed in 1862, built by the widow of the local MP, Henry Fitzroy. The building housed the private Lewes Library Society up until 1897, when a public library came into being. A short walk takes you to the small humped bridge over the Ouse, and a view to the south should remind you that Lewes owes its existence and past prosperity to its role as a port. If there is one special time to stand on this spot it is the night of 5 November. Lewes and Cliffe High Street, east of the Ouse, is then transformed by the distinctive marches of the bonfire societies, celebrating, amongst other things, the suppression of the Gunpowder Plot and generally manifesting an anti-popery stance. William and Gundrada would have been horrified. It is a raucous experience at night: jostling crowds, bonfire torches, bangers, drums and music, the smell of smoke and fireworks mixing with the odd waft of deep-fried fat from the burger vans. Not for the faint hearted but a memo-rable experience – and you have a year to recover from it!

Harveys Brewery, next to the river Ouse in Lewes. It suffered severe flooding in October 2000 when the river broke its banks.

Someone, somewhere, will know how many pints of Harveys, the local beer, are consumed on Bonfire Night in Lewes. We don't I am afraid, but we guess it's a lot. The local Harveys Brewery, which you can see from Cliffe Bridge, is the oldest brewery in Sussex, dating back to 1790. The impressive tower was added to the premises in the Victorian period, in Gothic vernacular style, and it is this tower and brew house that dominate the scene viewed from the bridge. Behind the tower stands the other half of the brewery, the Georgian fermenting room, cellars and vat house. With the slight smell of yeast in your nostrils, walk along the High Street, past the Harveys shop, until you come to a small passage on your left. Make your way along the passage, across a car park, ignoring the beguiling Dorset Arms, until you come up short against the slate-clad side of a famous Lewesian building: the Jireh chapel.

Lewes has a history of Protestant non-conformism and many chapels were established in the town in the eighteenth and nineteenth centuries. The Jireh chapel was completed in 1805 and proved to be extremely popular, with over 1,000 in the congregation by 1826. The interior was almost entirely wooden, with box pews and galleries. *Jireh* means 'to provide', as in the biblical expression *Jehovah-Jireh* – the Lord will provide. The chapel entrance faces east, and is fronted by a wide classical porch and a red-brick façade. Retrace your steps across the Ouse, via the Phoenix Causeway (a reminder of the now disappeared Phoenix Ironworks), and look to the south. If the sun is out you might get a glimpse of reflected light from the barrels of beer in Harveys' yard. Further on, at the bottom of the hill, you come up sharp against another chapel – flint walled with three latticed windows on the first floor and a tower: the Eastgate Baptist chapel. Built in 1843, it still houses a thriving congregation. Walk on up Little East Street, noting the fine terrace of nineteenth-century houses in Waterloo Place, again with that familiar mix of arched doorways, iron boot scrapes, white sashed windows, red-brick surrounds and grey brick walls, set off by some lovely daffodils when we walked by. Near the top of the hill, a converted chapel, once a Gospel Mission temperance hall, is now converted to residential use. And finally, our last chapel, the brick-built former Presbyterian church in Market Street, which closed in 1945 and is now a flea market.

By way of Lancaster Street we can, a little wearily perhaps, walk up towards the Anglican church of St John sub Castro, which in its current form is a nineteenth-century creation in early English style, of knapped flints and red brick. Its squat tower with castellated octagonal turrets have not endeared it to all, some describing it as 'ugly' and a cross between a 'castle and a barn'. It stood on the site of an earlier Saxon church, but there is little evidence (as yet) that it occupies the site of an improbable Roman fort. Walk along Abinger Place and up the small lane called Castle Banks – we stop here, the end of our journey. You should be looking at a barn-like building called the Maltings (a former malt house of the late eighteenth century) and a large earthen mound, known as Brack Mount. William and Gundrada welcome the stop too and sit down. This is the site of their first Norman timber castle in Lewes, eventually joined to the other castle mound by a masonry curtain wall. It is something they recognise. Whether the Normans (and no doubt conscripted locals) quarried the chalk to form these large chalk mounds has been hotly debated. Some think the mounds are older and could have been Roman burial mounds or even prehistoric ones. We want to ask William and Gundrada to see what they think (if anyone should know, they should), and we practise the question in some broken Norman-French. When we turn round to seek them out, only the empty bench is there.

SOFA STATS

Start the walk at Lewes Castle (TQ413100). The total length of walk is approximately 4.5km (3 miles). The elevation range is from 2m to 35m above sea level. Minimum walking time is one hour thirty minutes.

ONE BOOK TO LOOK AT BEFORE YOU GO

Brent, Colin (1993), *Georgian Lewes, 1714–1830: the Heyday of a County Town*. Lewes: Colin Brent Books.

WALK 3: MARCH

DOWN TO JEVINGTON AND BACK

IN A NUTSHELL

This broadly circular walk is right at the eastern end of the South Downs National Park. The views from this particular landscape are spectacular: across Pevensey Levels to Hastings, panoramic vistas of the sea, the broad expanse of the Weald to the north and back along the spine of the Downs to the west. There are 360-degree sensations at many places so practise revolving slowly to take in the different views. It is almost as if this special piece of landscape was designed by the gods of geology just so that people could admire the scenery stretched out beneath. And there is a ridge-path quality to your journey. You stroll around the rim of a natural amphitheatre, around Willingdon Bottom, dropping down only once to the medieval village of Jevington. You will see lots of prehistoric round burial mounds and traverse one of the earliest meeting places for farmers in southern Britain.

TIME TO GET GOING

Where to start? The easiest place is the Butts Brow car park, at the top of Butts Lane (TQ 580 017). We were fortunate: it was a sunlit March morning of needle-sharp clarity. Go southwards following the footpath, close to the scarp edge, past the large copse of trees that lean collectively away from the westerly salt-laden wind. Pretty soon you come to a slight and small round turf-covered mound – the unmistakeable sign of a burial or commemorative monument probably constructed from around 2000 BCE. We say 'burial or commemorative' because not every round mound, when excavated, has revealed evidence of human burials. There are over 1,000 of these round barrows in Sussex alone, and they tend to cluster at the edge

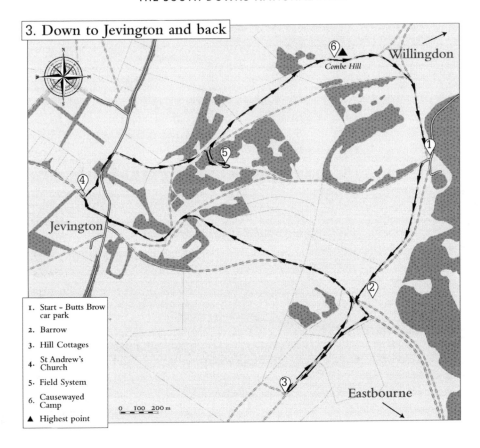

3. Down to Jevington and back

1. Start – Butts Brow car park
2. Barrow
3. Hill Cottages
4. St Andrew's Church
5. Field System
6. Causewayed Camp
▲ Highest point

of the chalk escarpment. Some barrows cover single inhumations, others multiple cremations that may have taken place over a long period of time, conceivably centuries. Most are chalk mounds, but some consist of largely flint. Some mounds were built in one endeavour, while others were constructed in phases. Some mounds are larger than others, and some have exotic grave goods buried with the deceased. Cremations might be contained in large ceramic containers, either buried upright or upside down. As you can see, the variety is considerable.

But why are these mounds where they are? What made some people want to have their final resting place here? And did everyone receive a barrow burial or was it reserved for some special section of the population? Easy questions, but the answers are difficult. Let's approach one of these problems from a different direction. A little to the east of this first barrow lies a rectangular plaque, on the turf. When we were there, faded red poppies lay flat and fallen to one of its sides. There are ten names listed, all Americans. They died on a cloudy day, 2 February 1944, as their bomber, badly damaged by enemy action, fell into the chalk hillside. These ten men were not buried here. Although this modest plaque records one terrible moment, it also transforms it. Those lost lives can be remembered today by those who place poppies. They can stand in quiet contemplation, removed from the everyday, looking out to sea or along the coast. Can we project these kind of feel-ings into the remote past? Surely the position of many of these barrows, invitingly tempting the onlooker to gaze to distant horizons, must have been bound up with repeatedly remembering loved ones, bringing comfort to the bereaved and transcending death itself?

Such sombre thoughts are easy to shed as you continue towards the sea, walking on such springy turf towards the top of a low hill, crossed by the South Downs Way. Once at the summit, close by the Ordnance Survey concrete plinth, is another barrow, this time broad and flat-topped. Why the different shape and size? Perhaps a family and a few generations of descendants lie beneath? Or was it someone of considerable importance, because the views from this spot are truly breath-taking? There is no one to ask. We don't even know *how* people were mourned 4,000 years ago. Frustration sparks our imagination and we conjure up grieving relatives. There, a little further on, past the dew pond: adults, chanting rhythmically, seemingly quite happily too, and some small figures, children we think. They murmur, arms linked; a few bend down, pouring something. We walk towards where they stood,

The flat, low burial mound at the summit of Willingdon Hill. The lonely hawthorn bends to the east before the salt-laden westerly winds.

only to find no trace of them, save for two more barrows side by side. A few steps more brings you to something more tangible and much nearer the present: the tumbledown walls of nineteenth-century farm buildings near the former hill cottages. The cottages were next to the farm and were requisitioned in 1942 when a radio transmitter was established at the site. Before that, we like to think that this captivating spot gave their occupants the longest of peaceful lives and made them the best of neighbours.

Retrace your steps to the South Downs Way, past an inscribed way marker that says 'Old Town Eastbourne', and follow the way westwards and downwards. We spy a colony of rabbits who suddenly freeze and then disappear haphazardly to the right, in the direction of a cluster of fields whose boundaries are draped diagonally across the eastern slopes of a hill. The banks look substantial, even from a distance, and must be one of the better examples in the South Downs National Park of an abandoned field system. But why the curious alignment, so much at odds with the natural contours? There is no immediate answer, so we head down to Jevington village and enter it past the whitewashed gable of the first cottage. Church first, perhaps lunch later – that's the way it should be – so we cross the street to climb to St Andrew's.

Jevington church is dedicated to St Andrew. Andrew, like his brother apostle Peter, was a fisherman, and the seafaring connections of this saint are symbolised by the unusual anchor cross above the south porch and nave roof. The west tower is of mid-eleventh-century date, while the nave is an early twelfth-century build. Most impressive is the curved wooden nave roof – a fine example of a Tudor wagon roof, complete with alternating hammer beams and king posts. There is a theory that some of these early churches began life as standalone towers, just housing a small chapel altar. They functioned partly as a status symbol for lordly prestige and partly as watchtowers. A late Saxon secular tower, which may have been a precursor to this tradition, was found at nearby Bishopstone. If true, this makes for a very different early ecclesiastical landscape from the one we imagine. But now we must return to more earthly matters. If you unfortunately find that you have plundered your packed lunch prematurely, which we are prone to do, despair not. There are three eateries in the village, including one that claims to be the birthplace of banoffi pie – 1972, if you are interested!

Walk northwards past the church and, a little further on, take the footpath opposite the pub and climb up towards Combe Down. The footpath keeps to the turf but on your right-hand side you will notice plenty of clumps of gorse – yellow-flowered in late March. Take time to walk between these, a little way down the slope, and you should come to the site of that field system. The earthen banks should be pretty obvious for they are over 1m high in places. Archaeologists call these types of field banks lynchets, and we presume they would have had hedgerows on top of them to make them effective barriers. Now lynchets, as the explanation goes, were formed when these small fields were ploughed, and soil gradually crept downhill, leaving the up-slope banks standing proud, while the down-slope banks got bigger through gradually accumulating soil. That's the

One of the way markers that presumably once signposted the way to, and distance from, Eastbourne.

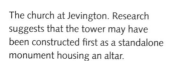

The church at Jevington. Research suggests that the tower may have been constructed first as a standalone monument housing an altar.

A close-up of one of the field banks at Jevington. They are substantial earthworks, approximately 1m high in places. Combe Hill, the causewayed camp, is on the middle horizon.

theory, although we would have liked to have been around to see it in practice. And another thing: these fields, which could be over 3,000 years old, only survive on this side of this particular hill. We ought to assume that these fields covered extensive areas of downland hereabouts. But if only these survive in this locality then the extent of levelling wrought by more recent agriculture has been colossal.

Regain the footpath and head north-eastwards. When we were there the weather began to turn for the worst – great grey darkening banks of cloud spread ominously from the west, the wind beginning to sweep across the turf. We quickened our pace upwards towards the near horizon where there are more mounds. It is weather for grieving. Distorted sounds carry on the wind. We struggle to catch sight, across all those millennia, of a circle of dancers, strung out like beads around one of those mounds. We head hurriedly for the northern-most stile and walk a short way through scrub to arrive at that very same burial mound, but there is not a soul in sight, save for some trampled grass around its circumference. Instead we find another quite substantial round barrow whose disturbed profile bears the hallmarks of some probable nineteenth-century interference.

Time to look and walk across the flat saddle of Combe Hill itself. Try to spot the slight but curving lines of earthworks and occasional entrances that mark the site of a causewayed camp, built by immigrant farmers nearly 6,000 years ago. Archaeological evidence suggests that these camps were built over a very short space of time, soon after the first immigrant farmers, with their families and livestock, had landed from the near Continent. They certainly chose their spot well. From Combe Hill there are spectacular views northwards across the Weald. However, these are not camps at all, but seasonal meeting places for feasts and exchanges, and perhaps thanksgivings for survival. For these pioneer farmers were, above all, strangers in a strange land, and that foreign feeling must have been stronger for the first few generations. Like colonial pioneers from more recent times, they had a need to stick together, to make lasting monuments in the landscape. Old uprooted traditions had to be replanted in foreign soil, just as much as new crops. People came together, dug ditches and made encircling banks of chalk, and through these organised ritual activities social structures emerged and were recognised: leaders, followers, close kin, distant kin. Their success was measured not just in terms of fields cleared and cropped, and animals reared and milked, but in whether their gods had travelled with them. There is no surprise, then, that offerings are sometimes found in the ditches of these camps. In the case of Combe Hill, three polished flint axes placed in a line were found in a ditch – axes that may have been used to fell the very trees and clear the scrub before the camp could be laid out.

Passing through the centre of the camp, and out to the east, you come across two very different barrows. First there is what looks like a 'saucer' or 'disc' barrow, a flat, circular space surrounded by a small ditch, but no mound at all. It is sited on a very ephemeral earthwork, with a north–south alignment, and has been viewed by some as Anglo-Saxon in date rather than prehistoric. Some 50m further on is another unmistakeable prehistoric round barrow, with stunning views down the coast towards Hastings. It is noticeable that all three of these barrows are sited close to, but not on, the causewayed camp. We suspect that even though a couple of thousand years could separate camp from barrows, the builders of the latter knew something of the special nature of the former and afforded it respect, or perhaps more likely, deemed it inauspicious to build on top of it.

Our final stop is yet another barrow, disturbed and slight, but clinging to the eastern side of Cold Crouch hill. Again the views are awe-inspiring, uplifting and transcendental. You feel a shocked humility as you sit on top of it and allow your eyes, and thoughts, to wander. Who would not want to be buried here? Who would not want to be remembered by such a monument? There are perhaps some more prosaic questions to ponder too – ones that archaeologists, good at describing and measuring and mapping, find harder to answer. Where are the farms of the first farmers – where are their hill cottages? And where are the presumably more numerous farms (and fields) of those who were buried or remembered by the construction of barrows? Was the downland around here a sort of sacred landscape, with settlements in the dry Downs valleys, or below on the greensand or coastal plain? Certainly barrows cluster on the north scarp of the South Downs and monopolise the viewpoints. But perhaps it was not so much that the dead wanted to see in the afterlife, but that the living, maybe down below, could see their ancestors? Or were the barrows built in the corners of the fields themselves and quite close to vanished farms?

So many simple questions, and indeed even more barrows, but many of the answers still elude us. It is dangerous to project backwards emotional perspectives from the present into the distant past. Yet you cannot help wondering if through barrow construction and barrow-centred mourning the sharpest convulsions of bereavement grief were not just a little assuaged by these unforgettable contemplated landscapes. If liberation from suffering is the mourner's goal, then is that more easily achieved here, on top of a seemingly unforgiving Cold Crouch, or down in the enclosed churchyard of St Andrew's? In which place is parting a sweeter sorrow? Time to leave this particular stretch of downland and head back to the land of the living by way of safe descent down Butts Lane.

SOFA STATS

Start at the Butts Brow car park, at the top of Butts Lane (TQ 580 017). The total length of walk is approximately 8km (5 miles). The elevation range is from 71m to 200m above sea level. Minimum walking time is two hours fifteen minutes.

ONE OR TWO BOOKS TO LOOK AT BEFORE YOU GO

Oswald, Alastair *et al.* (2001), *The Creation of Monuments: Neolithic Causewayed Enclosures in the British Isles.* Swindon: English Heritage.
Woodward, Ann (2000), *British Barrows: a Matter of Life and Death.* Stroud: Tempus.

WALK 4: APRIL

DEVIL'S DYKE, SADDLESCOMBE AND WOLSTONBURY HILL

IN A NUTSHELL

This is a fabulous walk along a celebrated section of the north scarp of the South Downs. The views northwards across the Weald are so fine that Constable (allegedly) was of the opinion that he could not do justice to them by committing them to canvas. The walk takes in three prominent hills: Devil's Dyke itself, then Newtimber Hill and finally Wolstonbury Hill. There are a range of monuments en route: prehistoric barrows, Iron Age hill forts, medieval churches and a Victorian farm and funfair. Also, uniquely for a walk in the South Downs National Park, the lurking presence of the devil himself paces in frustration up and down the length of the dyke – the biggest natural dry valley in the country, so geologists would have us believe!

TIME TO GET GOING

Let's commence our walk at the car park near the Devil's Dyke pub (TQ257110). The earliest surviving earthworks we can visit are those of a Late Iron Age hill fort. The earthen banks formed by upcast chalk from external ditches surround a roughly rectangular area of about 15 hectares. But if you walk around its perimeter, you will see that the banks are very different in size. By far the largest barrier is that on the south-west side, which presumably marked the main entrance to the interior. The banks on the north-west and south-east side are so slight and so far down the slopes that it's hard to see them functioning in any real defensive capacity. In essence, these banks delimit rather than defend. But what took place in the interior? We have very little to go on. A small excavation in the 1930s discovered

91

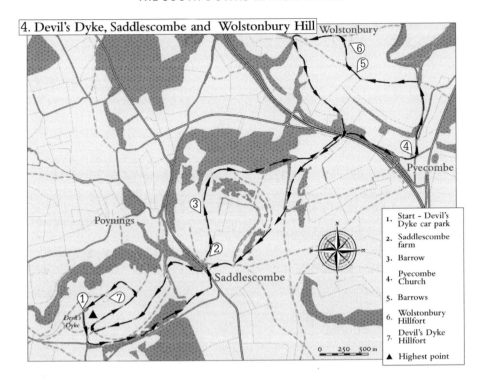

4. Devil's Dyke, Saddlescombe and Wolstonbury Hill

1.	Start – Devil's Dyke car park
2.	Saddlescombe farm
3.	Barrow
4.	Pyecombe Church
5.	Barrows
6.	Wolstonbury Hillfort
7.	Devil's Dyke Hillfort
▲	Highest point

the remains of a round-house and four small pits; these latter contained sherds of pottery, beach pebbles, animal bones and mussel shells. This looks likes a building where people gathered together to eat, but that's about all we can say.

Fast forward to the end of the nineteenth century and you will find yourself fighting for space amidst a crowd of some 30,000 people who are thought to have visited the funfair at Devil's Dyke on Whit Monday 1893. The fair consisted of two bandstands, an observatory, a *camera obscura* and a circular bicycle railway – all served by a train service direct from Brighton. In addition, for the thrill seekers there was a funicular railway ascent on the north side and a cable car ride across the top of the dyke itself – with dizzy views some 70m below that would have turned the stomach of the devil himself.

However, let's leave the fun of the fair, go back along the road through the hill fort entrance, across the top of the dyke, and take the path north-eastwards towards Saddlescombe. The dyke to the north gradually gets deeper as we walk along the top of the valley side. Folklore has it that the dyke was dug by the devil (actually we suspect by the devil's little sinners) because there were too many churches in the Weald and the devil wanted to reach the sea and flood the Weald with salty English Channel water. Of course, he didn't succeed, not least since the dyke takes a rather dog-leg trajectory and doesn't really head for the sea at all. There is even a mound at the bottom of the dyke that is said to be the grave of the devil himself. Geologists have a much more orthodox explanation, although one

The brick platform remains of the upper station for the funicular railway that once brought passengers to the top of Devil's Dyke.

Devil's Dyke, looking eastwards. The hill fort lies to the left, and must have made some use of the natural obstacle provided by the dyke.

that is just as difficult to imagine. Apparently, during a very long and cold period some 15,000 years age, snow lay on the South Downs each winter. The chalk underneath became permanently frozen all year round. In the summer the snow melted but not the chalk underneath. Melt waters then ran down the hillside, taking more and more saturated topsoil and eroded chalk each year, until the dyke took on its current shape.

A long descent past a dew pond, a modern reservoir and through stands of hawthorn brings you out on to a road and across this lies the cluster of buildings known as Saddlescombe Farm. Described as 'a little dimple in the Downs six miles from Brighton', life on the farm in the 1860s was immortalised in a short book by Maude Robinson, who was born to a Quaker family on the farm and lived much of her life at Saddlescombe. I read this little book in an hour sitting on a sunny bench one Saturday morning. Its prose is straightforward, honest and everyday – but provides glimpses of the ordinary lives in the 1860s that would be extraordinary to us today. The farm, now owned by the National Trust, has a long history, stretching back to Domesday Book, and was for a time was in the possession of the Knights Templar and Knights of St John. When Maude's family lived and farmed it, some forty people worked on the farm, which provided almost everything for life: water from its well, food from the gardens, wool from the sheep and even most agricultural equipment was made on the farm. The donkey wheel, which drew water from a deep well in the chalk, provides a direct link to Maude. The wheel was fixed to a chain which held two buckets – as an empty one went down a full one, holding 12 gallons, came up – and the job of turning the

Flint and brick buildings make up the majority on Saddlescombe Farm. Although quite close to Brighton, in the nineteenth century life on the farm, nestled in a fold in the Downs, must have been quite isolated.

wheel in 1860s was that of an old white donkey called Smoker. Just by the wheel you can still see one of those stave-built 12-gallon buckets and imagine a curious Maude struggling to lift one. She had been warned – Smoker was a bad-tempered old so-and-so and quick to bite and kick. Smoker now lies buried somewhere on the farm, while lying around are the occasional pieces of early farm machinery – all rusting bars and wheels like the skeletons of some extinct species – evidence for a not-so-distant past.

Strike northwards from Saddlescombe to North Hill on the top of Newtimber Hill. You circuit round the lip of an old chalk quarry, and if it's a sunny April day, spot the rabbits popping in and out of burrows on the chalk scarp. Known as a pest to Maude, because they ate the sown crops, some of their descendants at least have survived. Much more curious to Maude and her family were the traces of earlier peoples often found on the farm's fields by the agricultural labourers. They included a smooth, grey flint axe, a flint saw – 'a quite workable gimlet' – and a little bronze axe spied on a newly turned furrow. Maude even describes 'a pre-historic lady's china pantry' discovered when digging out a fox from a barrow on the very summit of the Down. We don't know if that barrow is the same as the one that crowns North Hill. Possibly not, as the most obvious barrow there now exhibits a wide oval depression characteristic of nineteenth-century barrow-digging.

On a sun-shining South Downs day the top of Newtimber Hill is a delight. And it is so for a particular reason. It is wide and flat on top and very unlike the typical 'whale-backed' downland hills that leave you precious little time for rest between ascent and descent. The views from it are spectacular, particularly back westwards along the north scarp, and down on to the village of Poynings and its cruciform church – the quintessential medieval village on the spring line below the Downs. Maude, out with her friends in a riding party, primly in side saddle, would have glanced at much the same view. Descend by way of West Hill, passing another barrow, and make your way across the busy A23 by way of the modern bridge. A short walk upwards brings you to Pyecombe church with its thirteenth-century tower, and inside the Norman chancel arch and lead font. When we were there the church was flowered for a wedding, and in a further spirit of enterprise it was clear that the church hoped to add to its flock by enticing in thirsty walkers from those who pass close by on the South Downs Way.

From the church, by way of its tapsel (centrally pivoted) gate, head due north-wards for about a kilometre, until you reach the second crossing of footpaths. Turn westwards and take a path which should take you on a quarter-circle route until you reach the summit of our last hill – Wolstonbury. Near the summit, but still a little distance from it, you will pass two barrows and a small, straight earthwork that runs across the neck of land that leads to Wolstonbury. Archaeologists label these 'cross-dykes' and think they are something to do with prehistoric land division, quite possibly to mark specific communities rather than any functional purpose. A few hundred metres further on and you reach the summit of Wolstonbury.

Now Wolstonbury is a monument that presents something of a puzzle. It's easy to see why it might be there – it enjoys such commanding views over the lower Weald – but it's odd in the fact that its encircling bank has an internal ditch rather than an external one. It is conventionally described as a hill fort and dated to the Early Iron Age, although some people have sought earlier origins for its peculiar form. Revealing Wolstonbury's secrets will not be easy, for the interior of the enclosure is like the moon's surface: pock-marked with craters. The pits that mark the hill fort interior were excavated, presumably in the nineteenth century, and – presumably again – the pit diggers were after flint. Almost certainly the flint was being used for road material, particularly as the nearby routes to Brighton from the Weald were seeing increasing numbers of travellers. It is curious that the pits seem, unfortunately for the archaeologists, to be excavated entirely within the enclosure. It is almost as if the diggers were granted permission to quarry flint, but only within the encircling ditch and bank. There are old chalk quarries too, characteristic of eighteenth- and nineteenth-century work, to both the east and west of Wolstonbury summit.

Our greatest admiration on Wolstonbury, however, was not for its prehistoric visitors or its much later quarrymen, but the ever so humble ant. Approaching from the east we climbed through a maze of thousands of small humps and bumps, each about 30cm across and 10–15cm high. It was as though the hill itself was suffering from some horrible medieval plague-like illness and countless sores pressed through its grassy skin. Our first thought was rabbits, but not a single one was in sight. Later research, courtesy of the Friends of Wolstonbury website, indicated that each little bump was home to a colony of over 100,000 ants. There must be some reason why they find this particular downland hill so attractive.

The summit of Wolstonbury Hill, looking north down on to the Weald. The outer bank, inner ditch and numerous anthills can all be seen.

Hollingbury hill fort overlooks Brighton and the English Channel. Golfing greens and bunkers now surround it. (© *airscapes.co.uk*) (Walk 1)

The town of Lewes from the south. Note the prominence of the castle in the centre. Keere Street is the upper part of the road running down the image on the left-hand side. (© *airscapes.co.uk*) (Walk 2)

The slight ditch and bank, running left to right across the image, that surround the causewayed camp on Combe Hill, above Eastbourne. The location enjoys views to the sea, but to the north looks dramatically out over the Weald. (Walk 3)

The hill fort at Devil's Dyke (on the promontory to the right) with the deep depression of the dyke itself to the left. The eastern bank of the hill fort runs left to right in the middle of the image, across the promontory. The Low Weald lies to the right. (© *airscapes.co.uk*) (Walk 4)

Looking south-west across the Downs towards the sea. The earthworks in the bottom left of the image are the remains of Edburton Castle. *(© airscapes.co.uk)* (Walk 5)

The impressive cross-dyke on Barpham Hill. The lone sheep probably stands on the counterscarp bank, with the inner bank to the right. The rounded profile of Harrow Hill is on the horizon in the centre. (Walk 6)

Chanctonbury Ring from the north-east, with its distinctive cap of beech trees. You begin your walk at bottom left, near the modern house. *(© airscapes.co.uk)* (Walk 7)

The windmill at Halnaker stands resolutely defiant on the summit of the hill, hoping for wind but ready for stormy weather. (Walk 8)

The small church at Chithurst sits in a secluded spot just north of the river Rother. Large quoins of greensand support the corners of both nave (right) and chancel (left). (Walk 9)

Looking east from Harting Beacon, the three lines of cross-dykes can be seen on the flank of the adjacent hill, traversed by the chalk-white South Downs Way. (Walk 10)

Not easy to find and even more difficult to photograph, the leaf-covered bank of one of the disc or saucer barrows can be traced in a circle at the southern end of Black Down. (Walk 11)

Looking solid with its square western tower, the Norman St Peter's church, here viewed from the south, dominates the Square in Petersfield. (Walk 12)

Viewed from the north, you can just make out the barrows in a line in the centre of the hill fort on Old Winchester Hill. Your walk continues southwards (top) down from the hill fort. *(© airscapes.co.uk)* (Walk 13)

From the bostal foliage, a framed vignette of Selborne. Just observable is the tower of the church, with the vicarage to its left. To the right is the rear of Gilbert White's house. (Walk 14)

St Catherine's Hill, Winchester, viewed from the west. The earthen bank around the hill fort can be clearly seen, as can the beech copse at its summit. (Walk 15)

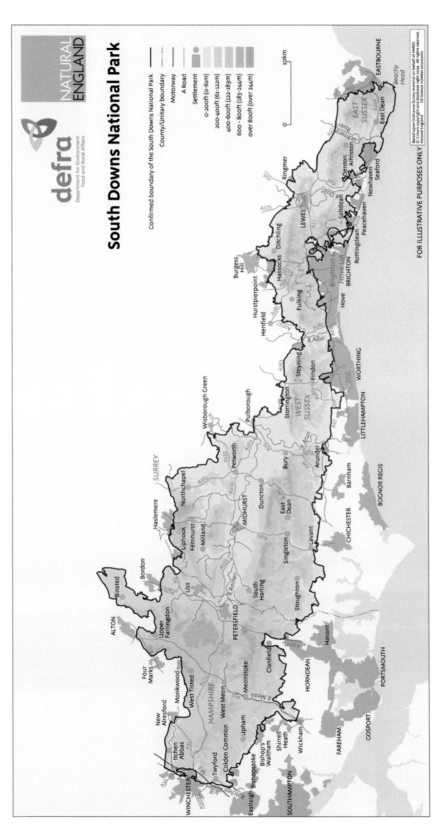

Map of the South Downs National Park showing the Park boundary, modern towns, major rivers and main roads. (*Courtesy of Natural England*)

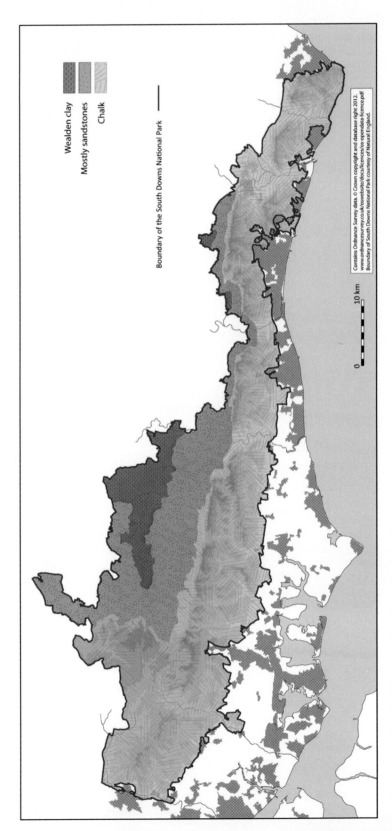

Simplified geology of the South Downs National Park. *(Courtesy of Dora Kemp)*

Wealden clay

Mostly sandstones

Chalk

Boundary of the South Downs National Park

Contains Ordnance Survey data. © Crown copyright and database right 2012.
www.ordnancesurvey.co.uk/oswebsite/docs/licences/os-opendata-licence.pdf
Boundary of South Downs National Park courtesy of Natural England.

0   10 km

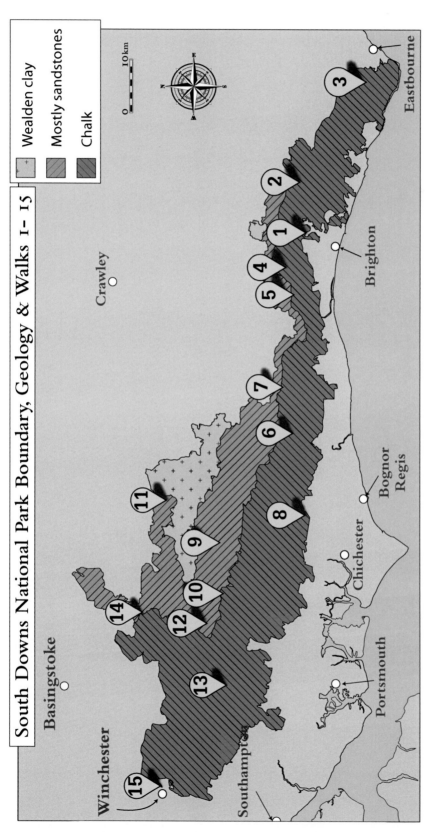

The location of the walks 1 to 15.

South Downs National Park

Location of some of the sites mentioned in this book

1. Abbotstone
2. St Catherine's Hill
3. Hazeley Down
4. Owslebury
5. Marwell
6. Hinton Ampner
7. Old Winchester Hill
8. Chawton
9. Selborne
10. Privett
11. Butser Ancient Farm
12. Uppark
13. Harting Beacon
14. Devil's Jumps
15. Bevis's Thumb Long Barrow
16. Devil's Humps
17. The Trundle
18. Boxgrove
19. Upwaltham
20. Barkhale
21. Bignor
22. Amberley Chalk Pits
23. Burpham
24. Harrow Hill
25. Cissbury
26. Highdown Hill
27. Chanctonbury Ring
28. Bramber Castle
29. Truleigh Hill
30. Thundersbarrow
31. Edburton Castle
32. Devil's Dyke
33. Chattri
34. Jack and Jill Windmills
35. Plumpton
36. Hollingbury
37. Offham Hill
38. Caburn
39. Itford Hill
40. Bishopstone
41. Black Patch
42. Alciston
43. Long Man of Wilmington
44. Combe Hill
45. Belle Tout
46. Pevensey Castle

Boundary of the South Downs National Park

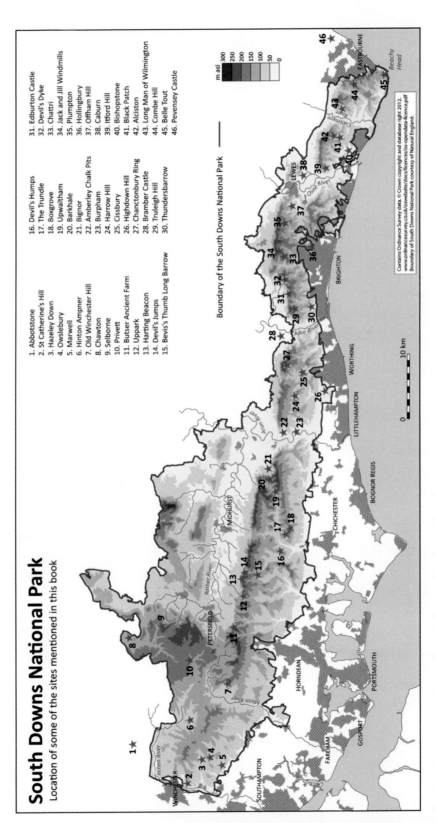

Contains Ordnance Survey data. © Crown copyright and database right 2012. www.ordnancesurvey.co.uk/oswebsite/docs/licences/os-opendata-licence.pdf Boundary of South Downs National Park courtesy of Natural England.

Location of some selected sites mentioned in the text. *(Courtesy of Dora Kemp)*

A glance at the map will show you that there are alternative footpaths to choose from to retrace your steps back, via Pyecombe and Saddlescombe, to Devil's Dyke. Most of the land is open access and owned by the National Trust, so do feel free to wander. We could not help noticing that the big square cross tower of Poynings church rose from the landscape right at the point that the dyke gives out on to the lower Weald. It is almost as if the Christians were mocking the devil himself – for all his digging, he couldn't even wash away the first church north of the South Downs.

You may be weary when you finally return to the hill fort on Devil's Dyke, but there is plenty there to revive you, not least the offerings of a pub within the hill fort – a unique combination for the South Downs National Park. You might have wondered about a rectangular, unroofed building just inside the hill fort entrance – the remains of an ammunition store from the First World War and a reminder of the social upheavals of the early twentieth century that transformed downland lives. But lift your spirits for the last time. If you do this walk over a weekend you may be lucky to see the paragliders launch themselves northwards from the hill, colourful sails carrying them aloft while they themselves are strapped and captured below like large cocooned insects. Gazing out on this improbable scene we wonder what Maude would have made of it. In her book about Saddlescombe she makes no mention of the funfair at Devil's Dyke. She would have been in her thirties then, and must have been curious about this late Victorian phenomenon on her doorstep. Perhaps her Quaker upbringing frowned on such contrived pleasures. She was, after all, rather bookish. As for the devil at that time – he had trouble remembering when he had last had such fun.

WALK 4

SOFA STATS

Begin the walk at the car park near the Devil's Dyke pub (TQ257110). The total length of walk is approximately 12km (8 miles). The elevation range is from 80m to 214m above sea level. Minimum walking time is three hours thirty minutes.

ONE BOOK TO LOOK AT BEFORE YOU GO

Robinson, M. (1938), *A South Downs Farm in the 1860s*. London: J.M. Dent & Sons.

TRULEIGH HILL, EDBURTON CASTLE AND THUNDERSBARROW

IN A NUTSHELL

This walk will take you from the scenic Adur river valley, just below Steyning, up on to the north scarp of the Downs. Choose a clear day for this outing, preferably one of sunshine after a couple of days of rain, because you need a washed and clean atmosphere to appreciate the extensive views as you gently climb. The walk will take you to three quite different downland monuments, all of them a little enigmatic in their own way. The first major monument you will come across is the Early Warning Radar Station at Truleigh Hill, a relic from the height of the Cold War of the 1950s–70s, and quite possibly one of the most recent bits of 'archaeology' within the South Downs National Park. A short distance further on leads to the curious medieval earthwork known as Edburton Castle. Your last downland stretch sees you head south towards the sea, down the dipslope, to the prehistoric enclosure known ominously as Thundersbarrow Hill. Your return to the Adur valley includes a river crossing to the lovely late Saxon church of St Botolphs. But first, time for a little cloak and dagger. Turn up your collar, get ready with your walking stick, and be on the lookout for anything suspicious.

TIME TO GET GOING

Let's commence our walk, innocently enough, at the High Trees car park, on the Steyning to Shoreham road (TQ 197 097). A short walk southwards and we join the South Downs Way, turning eastwards and walking straight up the slowly rising flank of Beeding Hill. Pretty soon you come to the National Trust car park, halfway up the hill. Make sure you take the opportunity to turn around

98

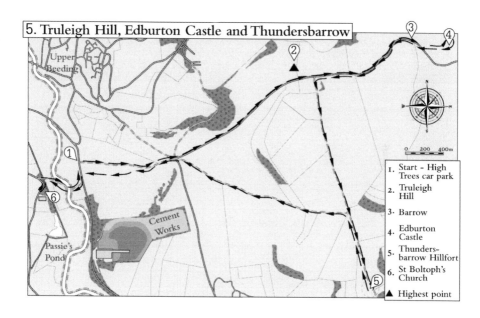

5. Truleigh Hill, Edburton Castle and Thundersbarrow

Key:

1. Start – High Trees car park
2. Truleigh Hill
3. Barrow
4. Edburton Castle
5. Thundersbarrow Hillfort
6. St Boltoph's Church

▲ Highest point

WALK 5

A view westwards over Upper Beeding, with Chanctonbury Ring on the scarp edge (left) and Black Down on the far horizon (right).

and admire the views. Spread below you, to the west, is the valley that carries the Adur to the sea. In that direction you get a profile view of the Victorian Gothic splendour of the chapel at Lancing College, a private school. A little closer is the chimney of the now abandoned Shoreham cement works and there is a tell-tale line of white chalk face visible, the southern side of its former quarry. Round to the west and the chalk scarp of the Downs continues across the valley, topped by the trees of Chanctonbury Ring, replanted after the Great Storm of 1987. In the foreground you might glimpse the masonry finger of all that is left of the Barbican Gate of Bramber Castle, although its surrounding tree cover is beginning to obscure both the monument and views from it. Panning round to the north enjoy the views of the northern limits of the South Downs National Park, and its highest point, at Black Down, and almost due north the distant summit of Leith Hill, on the Surrey greensand.

A narrow asphalt road then leads you towards some modern communication masts that you can see near the summit of the scarp. On the left, to the north, one of the numerous abandoned grassed-over chalk quarries punctures the smooth profile. In the bottom of the quarry you can still make out a circular path in the chalk, no doubt where empty wagons entered from one direction and laden ones departed by the other. A ragged line of pine trees leads you to a complex of old former farm buildings and three towering masts. Head for the one next to an innocuous brick bungalow and get as close to the latter as you can – you will find it deserted, surrounded by some heavy-duty fencing, and the entrance barred by a padlocked gate. Curious. Now, if we tell you that the entrance door to the bungalow leads not to a once-cosy front room, but a stairwell that takes you down to a 100m-long corridor which leads to extensive underground offices extending underneath the field to the east, your curiosity may turn to alarm.

The camouflaged bungalow on Truleigh Hill. Nothing remarkable to note, apart from perhaps the rather wide entrance porch.

TRULEIGH HILL, EDBURTON CASTLE AND THUNDERSBARROW

Truleigh Hill was an Early Warning Radar Station built in 1952 to replace an earlier one constructed on the site in 1939. In the aftermath of the Second World War, the West soon realised that the nuclear programme of the then Soviet Union was much more advanced than previously thought and the USSR went on to hold its first nuclear test in 1949. Numerous monitoring stations like Truleigh Hill were hastily established and were designed to provide warning of the approach of Soviet bomber aircraft, potentially carrying nuclear weapons. The underground bunkers were built to withstand a conventional attack and ensure that military staff could continue to exercise surveillance. The advent in the late 1950s of rocket-delivered nuclear weapons meant that places like Truleigh Hill, reliant on radar, became ineffective. The station was decommissioned in 1958 and sold to a private buyer in 1965. Such are the bare and quite scary facts.

But why the deliberately disguised entrance as a bungalow? What was the thinking behind that? Remember, when it was functioning as an Early Warning Radar Station there were six tall masts dotted around the site – not exactly inconspicuous. Presumably the military authorities wanted to deflect any idle glances from passing walkers about the nature of the activities taking place in (and below) the building. Perhaps the thinking was that too overt an establishment could have provoked potential panic, especially when some of the local population understood how little warning time might be given of impending attack, and how dire the consequences. Or maybe they really did fear that the well-dressed English gentleman, out for a Sunday afternoon stroll to Edburton Hill, could turn out to be a Soviet informer once the sun went down.

Just to make sure, we will follow him at a discreet distance, as he makes his way eastwards, taking the path that would become the South Downs Way. He sticks close to this path, pauses to look down the bostals or paths that run deep diagonals up the scarp, barely gives a glance at the prehistoric round burial mound just north of the track, but then climbs up and on to the summit of the next hilltop. When we get there he is nowhere to be seen. But what we find instead is another, much more ancient, early warning station, one built by people who had actually invaded – the Normans. The earthwork known as Edburton Castle is a rather unusual example of a standard Norman fortification known as a motte and bailey castle. This term is a relatively modern one used to describe an earthen mound (on which usually sat a timber tower or hall) conjoined to a lower bailey (courtyard) to one side. These castles, erected quickly with relatively unskilled or conscript labour, were built across northern Europe in large numbers from the tenth century onwards. Many of them, such as nearby Lewes and Bramber castles, underwent extensive masonry refurbishments. The Normans invaded in 1066 and Edburton Castle was founded soon after; so what is unusual about this particular site?

Well, two things. First, when you visit the site, and particularly walk over it, your experience is one of walking over a series of mounds, not just one. You also notice that the bailey, and particularly its outer bank and ditch, is located part way down the scarp slope. It is quite difficult to make sense of these apparent mounds, in the southern half of the site. They don't seem to form any coherent plan, although one of them does seem larger than the rest and presumably was the actual motte. So it is quite a shock when you look at these earthworks on Google Earth to see that they do, indeed, look quite regular and just like one motte, with its bailey to the north. However, appearances can be deceptive. We wonder if the 'multiple mound' feel of this particular earthwork comes from the fact that the Normans built on top of a prehistoric cemetery of round mounds. After all, the Normans did this elsewhere and the north scarp of the South Downs must have been littered with barrow groups. Also, we don't think the Normans were making any fancy claims to ancestral legitimacy by building on the remains (literally) of those who had gone before. They were, above all, practical conquerors.

The second unusual aspect of Edburton is its location. Norman castles were often constructed in population centres which often grew into trading towns. Again, look at Lewes, Bramber, Arundel or Winchester. Edburton instead must have been founded to look out over the woodlands of the Weald, to provide some early intelligence of any significant groupings and movements of men. If there were centres of Saxon resistance to Norman lordship, or simply bands of ren-egades who refused homage to particular Norman lords, then these were likely as not to lurk low between Wealden ridges or to conceal themselves behind stands of thick Wealden oak.

Before you leave, do soak up the views. Below you, on the spring line, lies the medieval village of Edburton; look further north and you can see Henfield to the left and Hurstpierpoint to the right, and then beyond that the High Weald.

The rather scruffy prehistoric barrow at Thundersbarrow. It lies just outside the gateway to the later prehistoric enclosure (to the left) on the hill.

To the east, a little along the scarp, lies the hill fort and Victorian pleasure ground of Devil's Dyke.

It is time to retrace our steps, slink warily past that ugly bungalow and take the track southwards, past Truleigh House. This long, straight path heads downwards towards the low hills of the dipslope and beyond to the sun-reflecting sea. You are heading for Thundersbarrow Hill, but as you reach the low point in the landscape look to the left, especially for an isolated brick-built field barn in the corner of a field, close to a modern electricity pylon. Field barns were much more common in medieval and early modern farming before eighteenth- and nineteenth-century rationalisations brought them into farmyards close to the home farm. Up the slope from the barn you should see three or four straggling field banks running from north to south. These are the principal field banks in an extensive system of much smaller fields that probably ran from the scarp slope all the way to the coastal plain. They could range in date from 1500 BCE to the medieval period, but most of these probably date from the Roman period, and some are associated with the people who farmed from Thundersbarrow.

Climb the slight incline to the hilltop. At first it seems there is not a great deal to see, so we start our packed lunch by way of compensation. There are extensive views of the coast and Channel, yes, and Shoreham below, but otherwise only a low nettle-covered mound next to some straggling hawthorn. However, if you walk around the west side of the hill you can see the curving line of an enclosing earthen bank. It is has been spread by later ploughing and is much harder to trace on the eastern side of the hill. Nevertheless, beneath your feet lies a complicated and ill-understood archaeological sequence. Again, let's begin with the essential 'facts', in chronological order. The earliest feature on the site was probably the burial mound – the Thundersbarrow – no doubt dating from around 2000 BCE. Perhaps a millennium later, a small trapezoidal enclosure was laid out on the top of the hill delimited by a small bank and ditch. This was succeeded by a large enclosure, the one that survives partially today, established around 600 BCE. Several centuries later a farming village seems to have sprung up outside the main enclosure on its eastern side, and was associated with fields, storage pits and at least two substantial corn-drying kilns in the Roman period. A trackway through fields seems to have led up to the main enclosure from the south-east.

Only small-scale excavations have taken place on the site so much is speculation, but what we can surmise, however, is that although the bigger enclosure at Thundersbarrow has been described as a 'hill fort' it scarcely resembles its much grander neighbours, such as nearby Cissbury. The hill it is situated on is very slight, and its enclosing bank was never held up by a vertical palisade; its accompanying ditch was also quite shallow. No traces of permanent occupation have ever been found inside. It appears to be more of a communal centre than fortification: a place where farming people (and animals?) gathered, rather than a place where they defended themselves. And another thing: the bigger enclosure, with its south-east-facing entrance, deliberately avoided the large burial mound and left it intact

Splendid in apparent isolation is the church of St Botolphs. Look out for the scratch sundial near the porch on its southern (right) side.

outside the entrance. On the face of it this looks very intentional and there may well have been an element of respect for an earlier place of burial. Lots of questions, then, and not many definitive answers. Take time to stand and admire the sweeping views east and west along the coastal plain, and spare a thought for the harvesters who some 2,000 years ago toiled all summer long on the slopes beneath you: corn-laden carts creaking along towards the smoke-surrounded drying kilns – it must have been hot work.

Now retrace your steps towards Truleigh Hill, glancing occasionally back so that you can better detect the earthworks of the Thundersbarrow enclosure. Take a left at the wooden silage stalls, and down and then up a track known as Monarch's Way. The fields left and right of you are so much bigger than the tiny rectangular fields that criss-crossed these hills thousands of years ago. Soon you reach Beeding Hill car park, and if your spirit still moves you, cross the main road, and then the bridge over the Adur, where a short walk brings you to our final destination, the small church of St Botolphs. This is the moment to relax, finally, on a pew in its cool interior. The church dates from the late Saxon period, and its congregation, drawn from a thriving port on the Adur, flourished in the early medieval period. Then nature in all its whimsical perversity intervened, changing the course of the river, and the port and church shrank in size. Look out for the little 'squints' on the north and south sides of the church. The one of the north side was probably a leper's squint, so those with a disease or excommunicated could watch the service.

On the south side there is a scratch sundial near the squint, quite possibly indicating times when a sinner could confess. Squints could have more overtly political uses, of course. During the Reformation Thomas Cromwell's spies might have surveyed services just to make sure all trace of popery had been discarded. The squint was an architectural device that permitted undetected reconnaissance. In fact, squints were just the sort of arrangement our well-dressed informer would have appreciated.

SOFA STATS

Begin the walk at the High Trees car park (TQ 197 097). The total length of walk is approximately 13km (5.5 miles). The elevation range is from 2m to 204m above sea level. Minimum walking time is three hours fifteen minutes.

WALK 5

ONE BOOK TO LOOK AT BEFORE YOU GO

Taylor, R. (2007), *Shoreham's Radar Station: the Story of RAF Truleigh Hill*. Privately published, but available from West Sussex County Council Library Service.

HARROW HILL AND BRITAIN'S FIRST MINERS

IN A NUTSHELL

Mining and national parks don't go together. But a very long time before national parks were even thought of, mines were a prominent part of the landscape you will walk through today. This section of the South Downs contains remains of the earliest mines in Britain – flint mines. It is hard to believe that some 6,000 years ago miners sunk shafts and pits on some of these hilltops, looking for the most valued material of their day: the black flint buried in horizontal layers in the chalk. I say miners, but we need to forget about images of more recent miners that most of us carry around in our heads – the tough, grimy-faced colliers who used to emerge blinking into the sunlight after a hard shift at the coal face. As so often when trying to imagine the past, the first task is to forget about the present. These flint miners were seasonal excavators, sinking perhaps just one pit or shaft a year, maybe with their families in attendance. Nor can we be sure that the miners were all men – women and children may have been equal participants. Along the way we will also see ponds, field systems, barrows, a chalk quarry, a cross-dyke, an Iron Age enclosure and, incongruously, a Second World War tank. About 200 generations separate us from those first miners. Several of those generations have left their marks on the ground for us to discover.

TIME TO GET GOING

Let's begin at the car park at Kithurst Hill, on the north scarp (TQ 069 124). When we set out it was a wet and grey day in late April, and it hadn't noticeably improved by the time we finished. But days like this remind us that the South

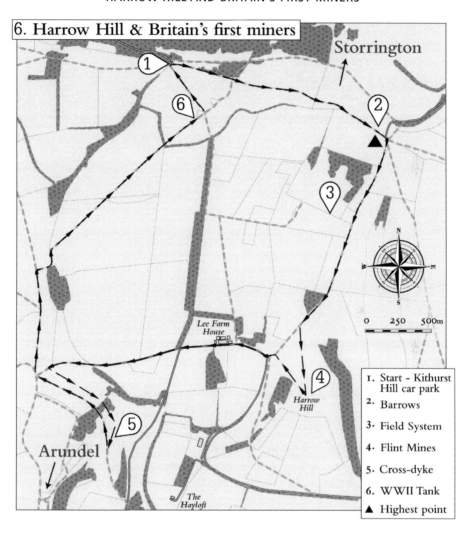

6. Harrow Hill & Britain's first miners

Storrington

Lee Farm House

Arundel

Harrow Hill

The Hayloft

0   250   500m

1. Start – Kithurst Hill car park
2. Barrows
3. Field System
4. Flint Mines
5. Cross-dyke
6. WWII Tank
▲ Highest point

WALK 6

Downs National Park is not all about sunlit turf, extensive views and wooded green hangers. For those who work the local land it can be, in its way, a cold, harsh and isolating environment. However, we don't have far to go to our first monument: just to the east of the car park is a grass-covered round barrow – a burial mound some 3,500 years old. Head along the South Downs Way towards Chantry Post. To the south, the field is a mass of bright yellow, planted with an increasingly popular crop: rape. Rape was grown in England from the fourteenth century onwards, and in the nineteenth century its oil was used to lubricate steam engines. Now it is used to provide animal feed and vegetable oil. Today, a few wet swallows skit along the tops of the plants. In the distance to the south, low but dominating, are the rounded Harrow Hill and to the east its neighbour Blackpatch. On both their summits miners toiled some 6,000 years ago.

Onwards to the east and past another dew pond, this one containing quite a lot of water. Soon you arrive at another car park at Chantry Post. There are a few hardy walkers out – all waterproofed and rosy-cheeked, no doubt thinking that they have earned a good lunch when they get off these Downs. But none of them look at the collection of turf mounds right next to the track. Admittedly they are not the most obvious barrows in the South Downs National Park, but let your eyes get accustomed to their gentle curves, albeit masked by thick-ish grass, and you can gradually make out a Bronze Age barrow cemetery. On a fine day there would be spectacular views to be had – southwards across the undulating hills and north-westwards down to the Weald and across to Black Down, the highest point of the Park. But today, under your feet, someone's mother or father lies resting beneath these mounds, so tread carefully.

Between the mounds there are molehills and they trigger a response from me that now seems as innate as walking or sleeping. When I was a young student studying archaeology one of my peers, who was much more knowledgeable, always used to kick over mole heaps when out on field trips, to see what Mr (or Mrs) Mole had unearthed. On the Downs they will sometimes throw out small flint tools, not wanted in their cosy burrows. So I spread one or two of these ones with my foot, but no luck. Now strike southwards, a long path straight towards Harrow Hill. To the right of you, as you walk, note some earthwork banks. These gradually become more obvious as you walk southwards: long strips of green running north–south in line with the contours. They must be field boundaries, and part of a more extensive system of fields that covered this part of the Downs. As far as we are aware they are undated; they could be as early as 1,500 BCE or date from the medieval period (there is a deserted medieval

A dew pond on the walk, looking southwards towards Harrow Hill, on the skyline to the right.

Earthen field banks of an undated field system run north to south down the dip slope of the Downs. The line of trees leading down to Lee Farm is on the horizon.

village not far to the south at Lower Barpham). They do remind us that an earlier pattern (probably more than one pattern) of trackways and fields underlies the modern one. Each generation fashioned a farming landscape to suit its particular crops, animals and working practices.

Make a detour from the footpath at the bottom of Harrow Hill and walk gently to its summit.★ The smooth slope of the hill gives way near its top to a cratered moonscape of open-cast flint mining, filled in pits and shafts. These are the now silent works of those early flint miners. Some of the deepest shafts had galleries at their bases in which miners could follow the horizontal seams of flint. Interpretation of these early mines is problematic. The flint was extracted using antler picks to make different sorts of tools, but perhaps predominantly polished flint axes for some of these first farmers. However, these mines don't always seem to have been sited to exploit the very best-quality flint, nor is it likely that these mines could have provided all the flint for contemporary communities. Archaeologists think that the landscape setting of some of these mines was just as important as the flint that was recovered. And, indeed, there is a line of early mines in this area – Cissbury, Church Hill, Blackpatch and Harrow Hill – all occupying hilltops looking southwards to the coastal plain and sea.

There probably was something special about the flint from these mines – but it may not have been about function. An axe from Harrow Hill may have been valued because it had been dug from the chalk at great depth as a result of what must have been a dangerous undertaking. It was an object to be revered, not used. Just like modern miners, these were a suspicious lot. Various chalk objects, mysterious signs on the walls of the chalk galleries and the occasional human burial suggest that the miners realised they had entered the below-ground world of spirits and gods. Something had to be given for what had been taken – hence the offerings.

On the summit of Harrow Hill, just to the west of the shafts, is a small rectangular enclosure, marked on the ground by a low earthen bank. This is much later than the mines, dating to around 800 BCE. It is hard to imagine this as a defensive

The cratered surface, caused by prehistoric flint mines, on the eastern flanks of Harrow Hill. Views across a heavily farmed landscape include the adjacent flint mines on Blackpatch Hill (on the horizon to the right).

enclosure, and indeed, when it was partially excavated, there was little sign of habitation. However, what was remarkable was the great number of cattle skulls and jaw bones found on the site. These could be all that remains of periodic feasts. Perhaps the spiritual nature of Harrow Hill had endured throughout most of prehistory and these distant successors of those early miners celebrated the traditional sanctity of the place by gathering together, enjoying a beef barbecue and drinking local beer every year. Life was not always nasty, brutish and short – even then.

Retrace your steps to the footpath and skirt around the west side of Harrow Hill. Before you turn westwards to walk through Lee Farm, take a look at the old chalk quarry to the east. In particular see that in the face of the chalk there are two grey horizontal lines, interrupted in part by tectonic uplift. These are the prized horizontal seams of flint that those prehistoric miners sought. We sit on a small spoil heap to eat our sandwiches, warming ourselves with sweet and steaming tea. The weather overhead is still overcast, and the surface of the chalk is now a sticky white wetness. It does not take much imagination to hear the cries of the elderly, mothers and smaller children from 200 generations ago scrambling up such slopes, levering out small slabs of flint and making scrapers or arrowheads to take home, while the more experienced dug the shafts on the hilltop. Imagine too the whiteness of the scene. Everyone, even the dogs, soon becomes covered in a dusty and sticky chalk dust, coating hair, skin, fur and clothing. Mothers cloaked through their hard work, elders scolding the off-spring for drawing white lines on their faces, dogs white and wondering. When it is time to leave they dust themselves down, then file off, still smudged, leaving whitish tell-tale signs in their wake.

Lines of tabular flint on the western side of Harrow Hill. Note how thin the turf cover is over the chalk.

The walk now takes you through Lee Farm. Just before you enter the complex there is a Dutch barn on your right, and, just beyond it, a large circular depression in the grass. Now dry, in years past this must have been a pond for the farm. A slight linear depression in the south-east corner suggests that the water was channelled into the pond from further up the slope. Walking through Lee Farm is to glimpse the industrialised aspect of modern farming. The buildings are relatively recent, functional and charmless. Huge machines for ploughing and spraying dwarfed us as we passed, their arms or wings folded back into themselves, looking like sleeping dinosaurs about to stir into life. It is sad to reflect that walking farmers are a declining species in the South Downs National Park – we didn't meet any. They ride these monstrous machines or hurry past in 4x4s. We amble on taking the footpath to the north end of Barpham Hill.

Striking south-eastwards up the smooth contours of Barpham, we look in vain for the signs of a round barrow that should be hereabouts. Some of the ground here has been ploughed and the remainder is a closely munched green turf. There is no sign of a tell-tale swelling that would mark the site of a barrow. So much of the Downs was ploughed up after Second World War, and still some today, that you fear for the fate of any earthwork. We can only hope that the grave diggers some 3,500 years ago did a good job, burying their kinfolk deep into the chalk, beneath the reach of farmers who would follow them.

The summit of Barpham Hill is marked by one of those concrete triangular trigonometric pyramids, or 'trig points'. These were erected in the middle of the twentieth century all over Britain, with precise co-ordinates and heights above sea level attached to them, so that the land mass of the UK could be more precisely mapped. Apparently, on a clear day, two other trig points should be visible from the one we are standing by. The gloomy weather suggests that testing this in practice would be futile today. However, to the north of the trig point, laid out across a narrower part of the summit, is a magnificent example of prehistoric cross-dyke – an earthen bank and ditch, with seemingly a counter-scarp bank along its eastern section. Some hill forts have slighter banks than this so it could be defensive, the 'inside' being on the southern side, or it may have simply marked off the highest point of the hill – the summit – as special or sacred in the past. If so, there is little indication as to what made the summit so special. There are one or two circular depressions in the grass near the trig point. They could be old dew ponds, or maybe flint mines that were never extended – but nothing definitive.

Heading back the way we came we can see contour lines of unploughed field banks in the field to the west of Barpham Hill – no doubt the remains of some earlier field system, perhaps even part of the same complex of fields that we observed earlier. While engaged on these walks across the South Downs National Park we have become more attuned to the importance of trees in the landscape. Not just because of the significance of trees *per se*, but because each tree or wood has something to tell us about past human activity – and some of that activity is rationally economic and some less so. (We think of Charles Goring and Chanctonbury for the latter.) So a glance westwards will take you to the very circular Norfolk Clump, standing proud on the summit of the next hill, and we speculate that a certain showiness and pride has something to do with its planting in the past. A second glance back to Lee Farm reveals something a little more perplexing: a very straight line of trees – running north–south – ends in a curious two-pronged arrangement that seems to embrace the farm itself. Even from a distance the trees seem to alternate in species, one more brown-leafed than its neighbour. We think the present Lee Farm is a fairly modern creation but the purpose of this arrangement of trees eludes us. Perhaps the overall pitchfork-like pattern has arisen by accident, over different phases.

Descend from Barpham Hill and eventually join the single-file footpath that heads diagonally and upwards, tracking north-eastwards across two fields of green growing crop. It feels like quite a long haul, but this path has been here since at least the eighteenth century so console yourself with the thought that others have trodden the same way as you, probably in worst weathers and not so comfortably shod. At the junction of two paths, quite close to Kithurst Hill car park, you stumble across something they never saw: the rusting hulk of a Second World War tank dragged to the side of the field. Apparently the tank malfunctioned in wartime and was never used in combat. Instead it was transported to this spot by the Canadian Army and used as target practice. Buried in a bomb crater after the war, it was excavated by enthusiasts some twenty years ago. Just as we said: every generation leaves its mark on the landscape, it's just that some are more enduring than others.

SOFA STATS

Start the walk at Kithurst Hill (TQ 069 124). The total length of walk is approximately 10km (6 miles). The elevation range is from 85m to 195m above sea level. Minimum walking time is two hours thirty minutes.

TWO BOOKS TO LOOK AT BEFORE YOU GO

Barber, M., *et al.* (1999), *The Neolithic Flint mines in England*. Swindon: English Heritage.

Russell, M. (2000), *Flint Mines in Neolithic Britain*. Stroud: Tempus.

★ Please note that for access to the very top of Harrow Hill you should seek permission, in advance, from the Angmering Park Estate on 01903 882220.

WALK 6

CHANCTONBURY RING AND THE RING-PLANTER

IN A NUTSHELL

There is this great story, probably not true in every detail, about a 16-year-old boy called Charles Goring. He came from a privileged background, living at Wiston House, on which estate the iconic hilltop of Chanctonbury Ring lay. He was born in the middle of the eighteenth century and was keen on nature. He had a dream of planting trees around the earthwork bank that formed a circle around Chanctonbury top. In 1760 he put his dream into practice, planting beech saplings, as well as some Scots pine and spruce, on its crown, and becoming known as the Ring-Planter. The story continues that he carried a bottle of water up the steep scarp of the Downs each day to water his protégés. The exercise clearly did him no harm. He lived until the age of 85, seeing his trees reach maturity, and praising them in a poem a year before his death. This walk will take you in the footsteps (more likely horse steps) of the Ring-Planter. If you really want to feel the weight of history, carry a bottle of water in your rucksack. We took a flask of tea and drank it on Chanctonbury Ring. Not quite the same, but near enough.

TIME TO GET GOING

Start your walk at the car park just to the west of Wiston House (TQ 145 124). We began right in the middle of that extremely wet May (2012) known ironically as the wettest drought on record. Chanctonbury Ring was swathed with low cloud which drifted along the wooded flanks of the Downs and the sky was a slate-wet grey. Heading eastwards along the foot of the Downs, we squelched past Great Barn Farm, noticing the small weather-boarded barn supported on eight 'steddle stones'

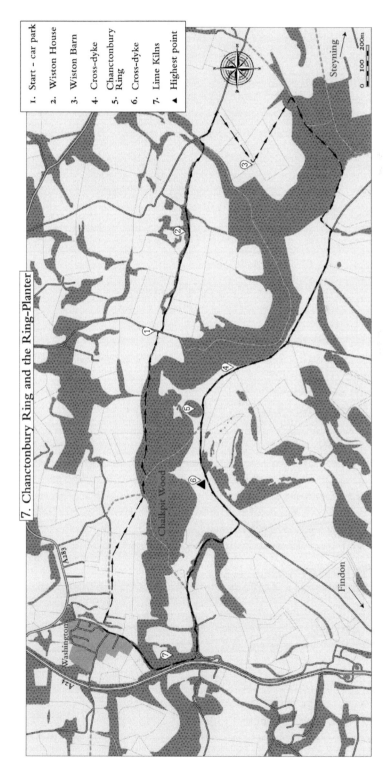

7. Chanctonbury Ring and the Ring-Planter

1. Start – car park
2. Wiston House
3. Wiston Barn
4. Cross-dyke
5. Chanctonbury Ring
6. Cross-dyke
7. Lime Kilns
▲ Highest point

WALK 7

The elegant brick piers and wrought-iron bridge that gives access from Wiston House (left) to the Downs to the south. Note the single arch for pedestrian traffic on the right.

to keep out damp and vermin. A little further on down the lane brings you to the first sign of Wiston House itself: a small bridge built on brick piers with a cast-iron walkway that must have taken house guests from the house estate across to the slopes of the Downs. This looks a later build than the mid-eighteenth century so we cannot imagine an earnest Charles striding purposefully across it.

Just past the bridge, if you climb up on the verge, you can glimpse through the trees the façade of Wiston House itself. Some of the present building dates back to 1575, in particular the great hall, with its splendid double-hammer beam roof. Sir John Fagge purchased the estate in 1649 and his great-grand-daughter Elizabeth became heiress to the estate in 1740. She married Sir Charles Goring, a neighbouring landowner, and the house has been owned by the Goring family ever since. In the mid-eighteenth century the house was reduced in size, with the demolition of the East Range. The south front, which you should now be looking at, was added in the 1840s. The house is not open to the casual visitor, but instead hosts conferences and weddings. From your vantage point you should also be able to see the square-topped tower of the St Mary's church, which used to serve the parish.

Back on the lane, continue eastwards along Mouse Lane (no, we didn't see any). By the second larger field, take the path upwards, beginning your climb to the wooded slopes. Pretty soon you will stumble upon Wiston barn, two sides of an old flint-walled barn, with several vertical air-vent slits. Continue eastwards to the nearest part of wood and take the footpath up the slope of the scarp. This has all the hallmarks of an old track, or bostal, on to the ridge top of the Downs and I feel sure that Charles must have taken this route some of the time. At the start of your climb you get surprised by another ruined flint field barn, but this one is covered by some well-executed urban graffiti transported to the countryside. The weather is still dripping and the wet clay underfoot is a cloying and slippery grey mulch making progress slow. The flask of tea gets heavier.

Quite a shock: urban graffiti in a national park. But it is a use of sorts for a former agricultural building on the Wiston Estate. MSK stands for Mad Society Kings, a Los Angeles based graffiti crew.

Emerging at the top of the path, you leave the warmer woods behind to walk westwards beside open fields. On a bad day, when the clouds are down, visibility can be restricted to a hundred yards or less. And this happens to be a bad day. As you join the South Downs Way, which will take you to Chanctonbury Ring, a dew pond appears just south of the track. Many such dew ponds were constructed in the later nineteenth century and, of course, they would have made Charles' heroic efforts redundant. Further on, just south of Chalkpit Wood, there should be a prehistoric round burial mound, but there is little sign of the tell-tale round bump which has probably been gradually flattened by successive swathes of ploughing. Your spirits need a lift – and they find one from a most unlikely source. Suddenly, or so it seems, the clouds lift, the air warms, the views get longer, and that famous ring or clump of trees appears on the horizon to the north-west. Stride purposefully towards the ring, but pause first by the anomalous modern water tank and fence – there are some important earthworks to understand.

If you linger long enough so that your eye gets accommodated to the local subtleties of grassed contours you will see, east of the water tank (and now redundant dew pond), the remains of a round barrow with a tell-tale diggers' depression at its centre. There are a couple of other barrows to the north – ever so slight rises in the turf – and I suspect a sizeable barrow cemetery once stood here over 3,000 years ago. But there is something else too: a curving length of bank and ditch which archaeologists call cross-dykes. Now, there are a good number of these within the South Downs National Park, and they seem often to cut across necks of land. They appear to be prehistoric in date, but probably had a variety of functions. I feel reasonably sure that this one, and its counterpart to the west of Chanctonbury Ring, probably carried ritual significance, dividing off the particularly sacred Chanctonbury space. Whatever was happening in the ring probably had some spiritual import. It is time to approach it and give our senses the freedom to explore.

The sunshine is brilliant now, as we approach, and seems to pick out every blade of grass in front of us. But what grass! Carpet-like, cropped and springy, it looks positively well groomed. But of the Ring itself – what do we know? Clearly the area gained prominence, in monumental terms at least, sometime in the Bronze

The ring of trees planted by the Ring-Planter. The grass in the sunshine has the feel of warm velvet.

Age as the slight remains of three barrows (there were probably more) lie in a line just to the south-east of the main earthwork. At the end of the Bronze Age, let's say around 700 BCE, a ditch was excavated around the top of the hill and an earthwork bank piled up inside. Our knowledge of this late prehistoric phase of the site is minimal: we have next to no evidence of what took place in the interior or whether the enclosing bank was reinforced by stone or timber; entrances lie on the north-east and south-west sides. For the Roman period we are better off. Two temples stood within the ring, one on the highest point of the interior, the other, polygonal in shape, on the southern side. Neither temple is truly classical in style; both owe much to native inspiration. There are deposits indicating offerings of oysters, cattle and sheep skulls, pig skulls from the polygonal temple, a few coins, a broken spearhead and one pin. When the temples were in use the perimeter earthworks of the ring clearly formed some sort of sacred enclosure.

That's what we know – but what can we imagine? The first thing to note is that pigs and boars were seen in the 'Celtic' world as symbols of fertility and war. All the fabled passions of Celtic peoples – hunting, sex, feasting and fighting – seem to be embodied by this animal. It is important to remember that in the first two centuries of Roman rule in Britain, most people were locally born and could probably trace their ancestry back to the island's indigenous, pre-Roman population. So we are dealing here with local gods for local people, those who wanted to cling to the old ways of worship and customary beliefs. We imagine that the ceremonies that took place within the ring were not always solemn – many of the deposits are probably the remains of feasting – so we think we should be able to savour the sweet odours of roasted pork and pig fat, smell the smoke wafting around the hill and hear the sounds of eating, drinking, laughter, as well as the occasional curse, chant, vow or prayer.

And another thing: ever since those saplings planted by Charles Goring grew to an imposing height, Chanctonbury Ring has been extolled by a variety of writers, including Belloc and Kipling, as being one of the quintessential landmarks of Sussex. The sweeping views from it, the distinctive vistas of it from afar and the sense of feeling lifted by a visit to it were captured in words by some of the great writers of the day. Just such an effect must have been created by the masonry and roof-tiled temple erected nearly 2,000 years ago within the ring. The tower-like central element of the temple would have been visible for miles around, calling people to feast, offer and pray, playing like a magnet on their hopes and fears. The worshippers at the ring probably came from the coastal plain or the lower Weald. A visit to these temples was therefore a pilgrimage; the climb up to them was probably just as important as the rituals within the ring. Just think of a group of families toiling up the scarp of the Downs, carrying food and drink with them, shepherding escaping children, while pigs slung on sturdy poles were carried across sweating shoulders. We sit on the warm side of the earthwork bank to have our lunch. I realise we should have brought pork sandwiches, but I keep that realisation to myself.

Step westwards from the ring and you soon come, near the path, to another round barrow – an innocuous swelling on green downland skin – and further on a slight bank and ditch surmounted by a single gorse bush, barring your way. This is another cross-dyke; in fact, it's almost certainly the twin of the dyke to the east of the ring. These two boundary markers must have bracketed the sacred space of barrow cemetery and later earthwork ring that constitutes Chanctonbury. Continue on, past yet another barrow and the local trig point, and you skirt another dew pond – this one called the Chanctonbury Dewpond. A sign informs you that it was constructed in the 1870s. It is now a Site of Special Scientific Interest (SSSI).

After the dew pond, leave the South Downs Way as it heads south-eastwards, and head across the top of a domed field, then finally downwards and through an old chalk quarry. Don't forget to glance at the two orange gashes in the landscape just beyond the chalk hills. These mark the site of sand quarries; this is a good place to remark on the different geologies of the South Downs National Park and their relevance for its history. Drop down right to the car park and head northwards, parallel with the A24 but on its eastern side. Incongruously you may come across a

WALK 7

Owlscroft Barn – all corrugated sheeting at the foot of the Downs. But the shape is that of a hipped barn and the timber frame is intact within.

life-size representation of a giraffe, just to the west of the path. Clearly it demands an explanation – but we haven't got one yet. No matter, just below the animal, and dug into the hillside, are the remains of a number of brick-built lime kilns that produced lime for construction work and agricultural use in the nineteenth and early twentieth centuries. Such kilns – and the dust, smoke, heat and noise that went with them – coupled with the processions of horses and carts to remove the lime were a common occurrence on the Downs and surrounding farms.

Take the path towards Washington but then turn east, past Tilley's Farm, and then diagonally closer to the foot of the scarp of the Downs. Like others before you, admire Chanctonbury Ring above. Feel at one with Bertrand Russell, who once remarked that 'any view that includes Chanctonbury Ring is a good view'. Perhaps not one of his most memorable lines but at least we know what he meant. The sun is still shining but the rutted chalk path beneath our feet is sodden from the morning rain. Soon you will come to another old chalk pit, grown over with a crowd of tall sycamores – it's a quiet amphitheatre of a place disturbed only occasionally by birdsong. On the other side of the track is Owlscroft Barn, at first sight a disappointing corrugated-iron-clad structure, rusting reddish and abandoned. But if you dare to take a closer look, a little peek inside, you are in for a surprise. Allow your eyes to adjust to the much darker interior and you begin to make out wooden beams, posts and boarding; in fact, it is a partially intact timber frame that clearly was once clad in traditional materials. You stride onwards, underneath an unseen Chanctonbury Ring, and back to your originating car park. Exercised physically and mentally, and spiritually elated, your particular pilgrimage is over. And that's just how it should be.

SOFA STATS

Begin your walk at the car park just to the west of Wiston House (TQ 145 124). The total length of walk is approximately 11km (7 miles). The elevation range is from 34m to 236m above sea level. Minimum walking time is two hours forty-five minutes.

ONE BOOK TO LOOK AT BEFORE YOU GO

Pennington, J. (2011), *Chanctonbury Ring: the Story of a Sussex Landmark*. Steyning: Downland History Publishing.

WALK 8: MAY

STANE STREET STEPS

IN A NUTSHELL

This is a walk you can be sure that many people have taken in the past, not least the soldiers of the Roman Empire. They marched in earnest from Chichester to London along Stane Street (Stone Street), but you can proceed at a gentler pace. On either side of this section of Stane Street are remains of earlier peoples – communities that had dug deep pits on Long Down and tilled fields on Halnaker Hill long before Rome became the superpower of the ancient world. Like the great novelist Thomas Hardy, you will appreciate that 'the Roman Road runs straight and bare, as the parting-line in hair'. Indeed it does, across this stretch of South Downs. But you will also discover the spoil heaps and shafts of prehistoric flint miners, and their burial mounds and hilltop enclosure on nearby Halnaker. And, while enjoying the glorious views from Halnaker, you will find traces of more recent industry and conflict – the miller and his windmill, the twentieth-century soldiers and their air defences from the Second World War. But first, that road …

TIME TO GET GOING

Start at the Forestry Commission car park in Eartham Wood (SU 938 106), north-east of Chichester. Walk eastwards a short way along the modern road, and, as the road turns to the southwards, you will see a footpath sign and a small but enticing gap in woodland on the south side of the road. Leave the modern road and slip through the gap – this is your Looking Glass moment – and enter an alternative world nearly 2,000 years old. Right beneath your feet is the straight-ish embankment of Stane Street. The ground falls away on each side, and its surface is bare,

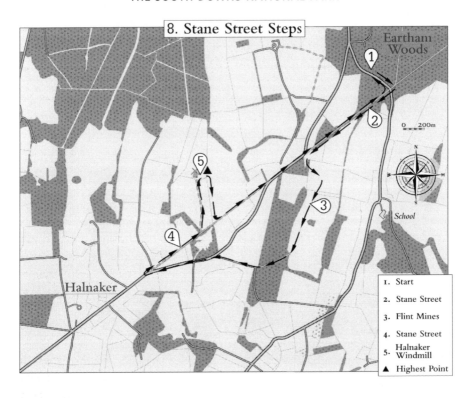

Stane Street looking south. This was the central carriageway and there would have been no trees in Roman times.

criss-crossed by old roots. The ancient road is hemmed in on both sides by stands of coppiced hazel, so its surface is flecked with May-morning sunlight, darker and cooler. Walk on and you come to a grassed firebreak, and then clear fields on each side, and you can more clearly see the raised ground that comprises the road.

Now the thing that most people remember is that Roman roads were straight, and for stretches they certainly are, with the army surveyors standing on one high point and aligning it on another one in the distance. But when it comes to inclines, such as the descent down the north scarp at Bignor, then a more gradual, sinuous route could be chosen, for the roads were not supposed just to echo to the sound or marching feet, but also horses' hooves and creaking and laden cart axles. Excavations of this section of Stane Street have shown that the road make-up consisted of a layer of clay placed directly on the stripped chalk, capped by large flints and then by a layer of smaller flints. The road surface was usually cambered and drainage ditches flanked both its sides. The overall width of the road was around 25m (about 82ft) and the raised section that you now walk on may have been its central carriageway for cart traffic. On one excavation well-worn ruts could be discerned in the carriageway, and these were about 2m (7ft) apart. Perhaps soldiers passed each other, steadfastly marching in opposite directions, on either side of the raised area.

As you proceed along the embankment, the ground starts to slope down towards the A285 and the noise of traffic gets more insistent. When we walked this stretch it didn't feel that straight, but checking the map assured us that it was! Stane Street must have been one of the earliest Roman roads in Britain, constructed sometime around the middle of the first century CE. However, there were probably roads or at least trackways in Britain before the Romans came. So spare a few thoughts for the reactions of local people. Most of them probably had only a hazy idea of who these newcomers were, less still that they were about to become incorporated within the Roman Empire; indeed, the whole idea of an empire was incomprehensible to them. While the army surveyors laid out the line of the road, it was no doubt slaves and conscript labour that was set to work digging and laying all those flints. And then, as now, having a new road driven across your community's land was not a thing to be welcomed. Historians in the past have often extolled the benefits of Roman civilisation. In the first decades of contact I can't imagine that many of the locals felt the same way.

As Stane Street reaches the modern road, under which it lies for a short stretch, go southwards across the field to the gate on the far side, keeping the tall pine trees to your right. Walk up and over the crest of Long Down before taking the footpath south-west towards a small copse of beech, oak and bluebells. Take your time to appreciate the views along the coast. In addition, to your west you should be able to make out the white-capped windmill on Halnaker Hill, where you will soon be heading. To the east lies the small village of Eartham, with its twelfth-century church (according to Pevsner – or more likely his co-author Ian Nairn – the victim of a 'terrible restoration in 1869' which greatly spoilt its exterior).

To the south-west you should be able to make out the spire of Chichester Cathedral and, on a clear day, the southern cliffs of the Isle of Wight.

Leaving the copse behind, step westwards down the slope, crossing the field boundary by a small stile. In a grassed field you should see some fairly large humps and bumps clustered together. These are the remains of filled-in mining shafts and their associated spoil heaps (just like the ones on the Harrow Hill walk), incredibly dating from nearly 6,000 years ago. There are over thirty depressions in this part of the field and during the 1950s a sample of the complex – two workshop floors and one shaft – was excavated. Now we do have to acknowledge here that this exercise was a collaborative effort between the human and animal kingdoms. Moles and rabbits, by way of their molehills and burrows in the field, were instrumental in guiding the excavators to the presence of worked flakes, and in the case of one historically minded rabbit, a rough out for a flint axe. The first workshop floor – where the deep-mined flint was chipped and flaked into small tools – also produced some deer antler punches which were used to remove tiny pieces of flint from the edge of flakes to give them a serrated edge. The one shaft excavated was dug to a depth of 5m (15ft), reaching a good seam of flint and also revealing antler picks and shovels formed from the shoulder blades of oxen and some chalk blocks with incised lines. At one place in the shaft a small mass of about 100 flakes was located, all apparently struck from the same piece of flint. This sort of evidence is rare and allows us to imagine a specific moment in past time when someone crouched in a shaft and spent five or ten minutes producing an implement. The second workshop floor was covered with the debris from fashioning a number of tool types including axes, knives, scrapers, borers and saws.

The grass-covered depressions masking the former flint mines at Long Down. Moles and rabbits have played their part in the discovery of prehistoric flint work.

Mill Cottage on the way up to Halnaker Hill. Stane Street lies underneath the track to the right.

WALK 8

Leave the flint mine field at its southern edge and walk south-westwards and down through a wood on the map marked Thicket Beeches. I must have missed the lesson at school when they taught tree identification but the path here seems to be elegantly lined with coppiced hazel. Emerge on Thicket Lane and turn right to go past Warehead Stud Farm to join the A285. We would have liked to have taken you a little further south to the former Boxgrove Common, now a disused gravel pit being filled and restored. It was here that the so-called Boxgrove Man was discovered in the 1990s – just a bit of leg bone which indicated a person who stood 1.8m in height and weighed in at some 80kg (about my height but some 5kg heavier), but most importantly, he lived almost half a million years ago. And, a little way further lies the early twelfth-century church at Boxgrove Priory, which is a fine mix of Norman and early English styles, so stop there after your walk if you have time. But this extended walk would take you outside of the South Downs National Park and the trek around the disused gravel pits is long and uninspiring. So walk south along the A285 (be careful of the traffic) before turning sharply almost back on yourself, up Mill Lane.

Once on the lane (and it's a relief to be off the busy main road), walk on towards the very pretty Mill Cottage, a half-timbered building with flint and brick and its own lamp-post, and then walk up the lane to the right. The track is sunk here between two embanked hedgerows, from which trees form an over-arching canopy, like a guard of honour providing shade on a day of baking heat. The gentle incline provides the opportunity to think back in time, for you are again on Stane Street, this time heading towards London and away from the coast, taking steps that soldiers of Rome took nearly 2,000 years ago, followed over the centuries by carters and their wagons, shepherds and sheep, and, in the not too distant past, peasants and freshly milled flour. You emerge from the shaded lane on to the shoulder of Halnaker Hill. Take the path due northwards and walk up towards our destination, the top of the hill, and its famous windmill.

Now, the windmill is obviously the stand-out feature on the hill, but there are much older archaeological remains on Halnaker. On your way up to the top of the hill, you will step across a small mound next to the fence that is almost certainly the remains of a Bronze Age round barrow. There are a couple of other mounds on the hill, now sadly ploughed flat, that suggest the hill was a focus of burial activity from 2500 BCE onwards. Again levelled by the plough, on the southern flanks of the hill, where you are walking, were once the upstanding remains of a late prehistoric and Roman field system. Agricultural activity on the hill has erased from its surface many of these ancient features, although it is a little (admittedly slight) consolation to realise that traces of the deeper ditches and pits will survive beneath plough depth. Reaching the top of the hill is the grassed island

Remains of Second World War installations on the top of Halnaker Hill. The famous windmill is to the left. All sit within a much earlier prehistoric enclosure.

on which the windmill stands. Much has disappeared from the crest of the hill too. There was once a large enclosure here, dating from the time of the first farmers and roughly contemporary with the flint mines; but all that survives today is a disappointingly small bank to the south of the windmill under the modern fence.

At least the windmill survives, albeit restored, defiantly waving its four sails. A mill has stood on Halnaker Hill since at least 1540, when tenants farmers were able to have their own portion of the harvest, or 'gleanings', ground into wheatmeal for their own use. The present structure dates from the late eighteenth century. It once had four floors and was turned to face the wind by a fan tail. Incidentally, you can sit inside it, back to its rounded wall, while you enjoy your packed lunch. A miller's cottage was built nearby, but the mill ground to a halt rather spectacularly in 1905 when it was struck by lightning. Close by the mill, in the grass, is a sizeable circular depression which is probably a (now dry) dew pond dating from the nineteenth century. The most recent archaeology on the hilltop dates from the Second World War. Four large searchlights were positioned around the hilltop to seek out enemy aircraft. They are octagonal structures, brick built with concrete foundations for the searchlights. One of these solidly built structures also contained a Radio Direction Finding Tower, equipped with radio-transmitting equipment and aerials. Their purpose was to provide a radio beam to guide Allied aircraft back to RAF Tangmere and other local airfields, and they were also used to detect the direction of enemy aircraft.

It is time for a little reflection as you walk back down the hill to re-join Mill Lane (aka Stane Street) and continue north-eastwards following the footpath/ Roman road, a short stretch of the A285 and then retrace your steps, again along on Stane Street, through the stilled woods to your starting point. Those first Roman Army surveyors who laid out this stretch of road knew they were not paving the way across an unoccupied or even thinly occupied land. They could see fields and farmsteads all around them. There were even signs of antiquity such as the burial mounds or flint mines, and I suspect some of the soldiers recognised the former, if not the latter. Above all, this was a landscape of people, and some soldiers no doubt initially bartered for goods with the locals. Some long-serving soldiers eventually learnt the local language, married local girls, fathered children and cremated some of their comrades on British pyres. It may not be the first tune in your head, but let me remind you of Kipling's *Centurion's Song,* lamenting the dilemma of a Roman soldier in Britain, ordered to return to Rome:

> Legate, I come to you in tears – My cohort ordered home!
> I've served in Britain forty years. What should I do in Rome?
> Here is my heart, my soul, my mind – the only life I know.
> I cannot leave it all behind. Command me not to go!

Amid the fighting, the conquest, the colonisation of most of Britain, there must have been also space for personal struggles such as these. Many soldiers never

WALK 8

retraced their passage back to the Continent, preferring to remain where they had spent most of their lives, among people they once regarded as potential foes and who had now become familiar friends.

SOFA STATS

Start the walk at the car park in Eartham Wood (SU 938 106). The total length of walk is approximately 8km (5 miles). The elevation range is from 40m to 125m above sea level. Minimum walking time is two hours.

ONE BOOK TO LOOK AT BEFORE YOU GO

Davies, H. (2008), *Roman Roads in Britain*. Oxford: Shire Publications.

WALK 9: MAY

TROTTON AND IPING COMMON – FROM HEATH TO RIVER

WALK 9

IN A NUTSHELL

This is going to be fun. For this is a walk through two very different types of land-scape: on the one hand, an undulating expanse of sandy heath and heather on Iping Common; on the other, we will follow, for a while, the course of the river Rother as it flows eastwards past the small villages of Trotton, Chithurst and Iping, each of which has its own parish church. Iping Common, conversely, is well known for its Bronze Age 'burial' mounds. I have put the word 'burial' between inverted commas for a reason which will become clear. What I want to suggest is that, although these two types of monument are seemingly very different, and although they are separated in date by more than 2,000 years, there is a connection between them. That connection will make you think about both churches and barrows in a slightly different light. So read and walk on.

TIME TO GET GOING

Probably the best place to start is at the car park (SU 852 220), south of the A272, and just off the minor road that separates Stedham and Iping Commons. There is an inter-pretation board close by, for the commons are managed by the Sussex Wildlife Trust, informing you that in past centuries commoners grazed their livestock here and col-lected bracken and gorse for bedding and fuel. Such grazing came to an end in the 1930s, however, and invasive trees such as pine and birch gradually took over, threat-ening the survival of heather and its associated wildlife such as digger wasps, nightjars and adders. The current mosaic of ponds, heather, paths and woodlands needs to be regularly managed to ensure the different ecological zones remain in balance.

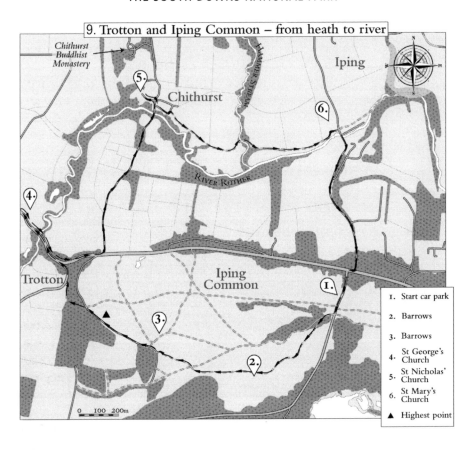

9. Trotton and Iping Common – from heath to river

1.	Start car park
2.	Barrows
3.	Barrows
4.	St George's Church
5.	St Nicholas' Church
6.	St Mary's Church
▲	Highest point

Take one of the footpaths across the heath, heading in a south-westerly direction towards the first barrow group located at approximately SU 849 216; it lies to the north of and across the road from Fitzhall Plantation. It was an oven-hot day when we followed these paths and the contrast with our other walks, mostly on the chalk Downs which we could see rising to the south, was immediately apparent. The sandy paths, derived ultimately from the underlying sandstone, felt warm and yielding, moulding to our feet with each placed step, preserving our footprints as we walked on – so different from the hard and, by comparison, quite cold chalk. If we had to spend a night asleep on one of these surfaces we would much prefer the heathland sands – a sort of naturally undulating bedding rather than the plank-like qualities of the thin downland turf.

The second point of contrast with the downland walks lies in the restricted views. When on the Downs it is relatively easy to get your bearings – climb the nearest summit, check out the location of the sea to the south, the villages below the north scarp, the other hills in the vicinity and you pretty much have a good idea of where you are. So much so that consulting a compass or getting out your GPS feels like the excess of a technophile. On the greensand heaths, however, views are more constrained, summits not so distinctive, the landscape is flatter and the vegetation mosaic the same in many directions, so it would be relatively easy to lose one's way, certainly on a larger common than Iping.

From where you are standing you should be able to see at least one substantial heather-covered mound – a Bronze Age barrow. As you wander around this area take a little time to 'get your eye in'. Do take care as you walk through the heather as it can conceal all sorts of animal burrows and getting your leg suddenly stuck down one will cause embarrassment (or worse) to yourself and alarm to any companion. After a while you will appreciate that the heather mantle covers at least three or four other mounds, and they seem to line up in a roughly east–west direction. Elsewhere in the South Downs National Park – particularly near Treyford on the north scarp of the Downs – some archaeologists have suggested that certain lines of barrows could have been sited with respect to solstices or equinoxes. This could well be the case here. One of the furthest barrows to the west is distinctively covered in green turf, which must, I think, have been deliberately planned and managed.

Now here are the interesting bits. These Bronze Age barrows are conventionally described as 'burial mounds' and most were constructed between, say, 2100 BCE and 1200 BCE. There are over a thousand of them on the chalk lands within the South Downs National Park. But these examples on Iping Common are on the greensand and the latest thinking suggests that these monuments were constructed as part of a pioneering phase of pastoral and agricultural activity that spread northwards away from the Downs in around 1500 BCE.

A Bronze Age barrow on Stedham Common. Covered in turf, it is easy to spot surrounded by heather.

A second point of interest, and indeed surprise, is that many of them, when excavated, have proven to be devoid of burials. At West Heath, some 5km (3 miles) west of Iping, a group of nine mounds was excavated by a good friend of ours, Peter Drewett. Nine mounds were examined, but only two of them provided evidence for burials, consisting in both cases of cremated remains in ceramic pots. There is a distinct possibility, therefore, that at least some of these barrows, both on the greensand and on the chalk, were not burial mounds but places of assembly where groups conducted collective rituals or ceremonies.

A third and final talking point concerns their manner of construction. In most cases the turf was stripped from the ground first and a resulting turf stack was piled up, which was subsequently covered by loose sand and gravel. Presumably, therefore, there were a few grassy areas for grazing stock. Nevertheless, mounds capped in these sandy materials cannot have been very stable, and the suggestion from West Heath is that they were revetted or held together by a circle of hurdles or wattles, perhaps made from hazel. Their appearance on the landscape would therefore have been drum-like rather than mound-like.

Before we leave these mounds, take a glance northwards and you will see a narrow green strip of land running southwards, between the birch trees, towards the barrows. This marks the line of the Roman road between Chichester in Sussex and Silchester in Hampshire. Excavation at nearby Brooks Farm, some 1.5km (1 mile) south of Iping Common demonstrated that the road surface was about 7m wide and composed of small flint nodules presumably brought from the Downs. Parallel drainage ditches flanked the road. The interesting question, though, is the relationship between the road and the much earlier barrows. I suspect that the military engineers who surveyed this stretch of road probably used the barrows as a marker, sighting the line of their road from a distance away on the prominent barrows. But does that Roman road go between the barrows (on a piece of flat ground), around the barrows (and to the east) or did they flatten a barrow to lay the road? I would like to think that, showing some sensitivity to the locals, the middle option was chosen, but the dense heather cover makes it difficult to be certain.

Head north-westwards now, along one of the sandy paths through the heather, and you should climb gently towards another ridge (SU 843 218) where there is another group of heather-covered barrows. These seem to be aligned along the contour, which runs from south-west to north-east, but from the top of them you enjoy fine views south towards the Downs and north-east across the top of the greensand plateau or ridge. At least one of these barrows was 'excavated' by antiquarians, the characteristic dished hollow in the centre being readily apparent. There is a great profusion of plants on the barrows: mostly purplish heather but some larger clumps of gorse – all browns and yellows.

Re-join the main path and follow it north-westwards as it curves along the northern side of Goldrings Warren. The wood to your left has a fine example of a woodland bank running along the edge of it. Some of the trees appear to be sweet chestnut, apparently introduced by the Romans, and which is now planted commercially.

Its timber can be used for fencing and the manufacture of those useful and delightful Sussex baskets known as *trugs*. The 'warren' element in the place name presumably refers to the number of rabbit burrows, conceivably some raised in the medieval period for meat or fur. And there are other barrows lurking among the trees. As for the Goldrings – well, we kept our eyes glued to the path but didn't notice a single one.

Emerging from the commons on to the A272 by The Keepers Arms (built sometime in the 1600s), walk carefully north-westwards down the busy A272 to reach Trotton Bridge. This fine but narrow sandstone bridge, with its five arches and massive cutwaters on the south side, has spanned the Rother since about 1600 CE. Walk on a little and you soon come to Trotton church, dedicated to St George. The church, built largely of sandstone, is fine enough, with a tower dating from around 1230 and the main nave from about 1300. But there are two fascinating aspects to its interior.

The first is that the church contains tombs and brasses that strongly associated the building with the leading families of their respective days: the Camoys of the fourteenth and fifteenth centuries, the Lewknors of the sixteenth and seventeenth centuries and the Alcocks of the eighteenth century. It is very hard to escape the thought that the church is less a shrine to God than one to the most important

The tomb of Lord Camoys (d. 1419) is difficult to ignore, right in front of the altar in the church at Trotton.

families of the past. The poor and humble parishioner, kneeling in the sight of God, probably felt more keenly the obvious presence of the Great and the Good. No more so than when Lord Camoys, who died in March 1419 and who had commanded a section of the victorious English Army at Agincourt, was laid to rest in a magnificent tomb right in front of the altar. The covering brass shows him with his second wife.

The second dramatic element in the church interior is the wall painting on the inside west wall. This dates from the fourteenth century and shows, in the centre, the Last Judgement, with, on either side, the Seven Acts of Mercy and the Seven Deadly Sins. Their fragmentary survival demonstrates once again how garishly colourful the interiors of some of these churches were before the whitewashers of the Reformation got to work. (The whitewash here, incidentally, was removed in 1904.) The Acts of Mercy – for the hungry, thirsty, naked and sick, amongst others – seem to have survived better than the Deadly Sins, which seems like a good enough reason to suspect that divine intervention still works in mysterious ways.

Retrace careful steps across Trotton Bridge and take the first footpath on your left. Head north-eastwards, keeping the river Rother on your left, and then join a small lane and turn north towards Chithurst. Cross the bridge over the Rother and the small, two-cell church of St Mary sits a little above you, to your left.

The height is important because some have claimed that the mound on which the church was built is part natural and part artificial, perhaps being the remains of a prehistoric or Saxon burial mound, or a Saxon or Norman fort designed to protect the ford. The church itself, originally dedicated to St Nicholas, patron saint of sailors and children, seems to date from around 1080. It was built of local ochre-coloured sandstone, probably quarried about 1km (half a mile) to the north.

Opposite the church, continue walking along the

Steddle stones, to keep out vermin, support this barn just north of the river Rother. The corrugated sheeting may well conceal an earlier timber structure.

An elegant little bridge on a footpath across one of the tributaries of the river Rother.

footpath on the north bank of the Rother. You pass a small corrugated barn, supported on 'steddle stones', and a sandstone field barn with air vents in the wall, and cross the Hammer stream by way of a wooden-slatted bridge with metal railings. This stream flows south from Hammer pond, the site of an ironworking forge in the early seventeenth century, and part of the Wealden industrial revolution which provided iron for armies, navies, coastal fortifications and domestic fixtures and fittings. Then stride on across a field to the church at Iping. This, the last of the churches encountered on our present walk, was constructed in 1885, although deliberately in the style of the thirteenth century. Once you know this you can appreciate that it looks much more solid than our two earlier churches. Follow the lane to the south, crossing the river by the seventeenth century narrow stone bridge of five ribbed arches; there are four pointed cutwaters on both upstream and downstream sides. Carefully cross the busy A272 and return to your starting point on Iping Common.

Before you leave these two worlds – one of heather, pools, birch trees and barrows, the other of bridges, rivers and churches – just take a moment to ponder the connections, especially between barrow and church, separated in time by 2,000 years and by the rupture in beliefs between paganism and Christianity. We were struck by the fact that not all barrows were burial monuments – that they may have been places for communities to come together and conduct rituals, some of which may well have involved prayer and worship. And, conversely, not all churches were exclusively places for praying to God. Some churches, like that at Trotton, seem equally to concern themselves with displaying tombs of successive generations of the aristocracy – the monumental memorials to ancestral lineages. With the sun still hot in the sky, the rippling heat haze seemed like a meteorological metaphor for the blurring of barrow and church, church and barrow. Time for us to flee into The Keeper's Arms. There, I told you that would be fun!

WALK 9

SOFA STATS

Start the walk at car park (SU 852 220), south of the A272. The total length of walk is approximately 5.5km (3.5 miles). The elevation range is from 28m to 58m above sea level. Minimum walking time is one hour thirty minutes.

ONE OR TWO BOOKS TO LOOK AT BEFORE YOU GO

Woodward, A. (2000), *British Barrows: a Matter of Life and Death*. Stroud: Tempus.
Strong, R. (2008), *A Little History of the English Country Church*. London: Vintage Books.

WALK 10: JUNE

HARTING DOWN TO …
WEST VIRGINIA

IN A NUTSHELL

Harting Down is owned by the National Trust. It is a Site of Special Scientific Interest covered with unspoiled chalk grassland on and among which flourishes a rich variety of plant, insect and animal life, including juniper scrub and yew, the carpenter bee and the yellow meadow ant. It also has a variety of archaeological sites including cross-dykes, a hill fort, a signalling station, dew ponds and a monumental folly of a tower known as the Vandalia Tower. There are magnificent views to be had across the upper reaches of the Rother, to the sandstones beyond, to Black Down and to the Isle of Wight and Portsmouth to the south. Some way back from the scarp edge lies Telegraph House, once the home of Bertrand Russell – philosopher, historian and social critic – and his wife Dora, who together set up a private school in the buildings in 1927. You may be wondering about the 'West Virginia' bit in the title. Don't worry – we won't be walking that far! But our colonial adventure in America will feature at the end of the walk.

TIME TO GET GOING

Make a start from the car park just to the east of the B2141 at the top of the hill (roughly SU 790 180). When we set out, walking eastwards along the South Downs Way we soon realised there was competition: quite a lot of earnest runners, all seemingly intent on jogging from Winchester to Eastbourne, passing us intermittently, sometimes singly, occasionally in couples. We wished a few of them good luck; they grunted and grimaced in return. Once we got into a muddle by a puddle at a gate, having tried to open it to let a runner through but then slipped,

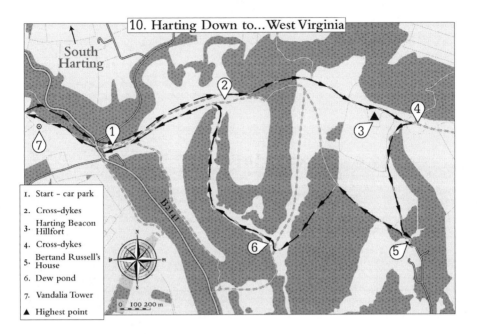

10. Harting Down to... West Virginia

Key:
1. Start - car park
2. Cross-dykes
3. Harting Beacon Hillfort
4. Cross-dykes
5. Bertand Russell's House
6. Dew pond
7. Vandalia Tower
▲ Highest point

the gate clattering shut just before she arrived. We got a stony look and walked onwards in sheepish and repentant silence.

The weather was exceptionally good for this June day, and you do need a good day for this walk to appreciate the views. We had undertaken the majority of these walks during the so-called wettest drought in history. We were used to low cloud, fleeting sunshine and a very English sort of humid drizzle. Now it was impossible to turn on the radio without news of another hose-pipe ban being lifted. It was all the fault of the jet stream, apparently dislodged and flowing much too far to the south. Miraculously today there had been a diversion. We wondered whether Bertrand Russell had said anything memorable about the weather.

Walk to the edge of the scarp and take in the views. To the north-west, below, you should see the village of South Harting with its copper-roofed church spire, then beyond a small hill on which lies Torberry Iron Age hill fort. A little further and to the west is Petersfield and further still the rising sandstone hills towards Selborne. Looking back, you might see the ruined stub of the Vandalia Tower – that is where we end our walk.

On the first summit is a small copse. We can't decide whether the trees are sweet chestnut or ash, or neither. There is a nice rustic-looking bench with a view on the north side of the trees. But we both agree it's sadly too early for a snack and stride on, proud and principled, eastwards and downwards along the South Downs Way. You will see in front of you, at almost the lowest point, a series of parallel linear features running north–south across the way and seemingly barring your path. On closer inspection these are multiple banks and ditches called cross-dykes. We have

A magnificent view down to the village of South Harting and beyond to the low hill (mid-right) on which lies the hill fort of Torberry.

met some before on our walks, notably near Chanctonbury Ring. These dykes are generally prehistoric in date and the orthodox explanation is that they had some function in controlling people or livestock. Indeed, the National Trust interpretation board in the car park offers this same functional rationale. I don't think this explanation is likely: if they are a prehistoric method of crowd or stock control why have multiple lines so close to one another? Think about it as we move on.

On the next little chalk summit you get a good view eastwards of Beacon Hill, and the western bank or rampart of the hill fort, running parallel below its summit, curving round to make a corner at its southern end. We descend into a dry valley that runs southwards. There is an earthwork near the scarp edge, perhaps a medieval or post-medieval animal pen. From it, a track, or bostal, makes it way down the chalk escarpment. You should see a four-way footpath marker set in a fancy stone plinth, and what looks like a trackway running at an angle up the hillside below the fort. When we were there, and much to our disgust, the runners were all heading south, down the South Downs Way, while we had to toil up the western slopes of Beacon Hill. By the time we passed through the low grass-covered bank of Harting Beacon hill fort, just beyond the gate, we felt justifiably smug. Pausing to rest, and looking back westwards along the Downs, there is a curious circular fenced construction above the tree line. It is too distant to get any sense of what it might be, but the fence wood looks bright and recent.

The hill fort of Harting Beacon from the west. The earthwork bank or rampart of the fort slopes down from left to right, before turning eastwards across the spine of the hill.

Make for the trig point on the highest part of the hill. There is much to relate so do lean on it if you want to. You stand in the northern part of a large hill fort, roughly shaped like a rectangle, bounded on three sides by a surviving bank, the north side formed by the steep scarp of the Downs. The area enclosed is about 12 hectares, and excavations and finds suggest that the fort dates from the Early Iron Age (i.e. about 700 BCE). However, the discoveries on the hill paint a perplexing picture. An isolated find of bronze implements in 1909 probably indicates that the hill was special in some way in the Bronze Age. There have been other curious finds: human skulls, two gold rings and fragments of a saddle quern. Excavations in the south-eastern corner of the interior revealed four four-posters and one six-poster (small roofed buildings that might be granaries), plus three tiny pits and a small quantity of pottery. The essential thing is that archaeologists have not found much in the way of what could be described as domestic refuse. It looks as if Harting Beacon was a big, largely empty space. The last excavator (Owen Bedwin) suggested it might have functioned as a stock enclosure, but this explanation smacks of frustrated desperation. I sympathise with that but think the suggestion is unlikely. After all, Iron Age people had lots of perfectly good stock enclosures – they were called fields! Despite what the National Trust board in the car park says, no Iron Age round-houses have yet been located in Harting Beacon.

There is more archaeology, however, on the hill. At least one Saxon coin has been found there and the small barrow in the south-east corner of the fort has been proven to be Saxon in date. There are several Saxon barrows in the South Downs National Park and they probably covered single inhumations. Sadly, the one on Harting Beacon looks as though it has been ploughed flat. But right where you are, by the trig pillar, are remains of much more recent archaeology. If you walk around a little you may be able to make out the small earthwork surrounds of a rectangular enclosure. A wooden hut must have stood here at the start of the nineteenth century, and a shutter telegraph signalling tower (see Walk 11 for a short explanation) to relay messages from the Admiralty in London to the fleet in Portsmouth. This system was remarkably efficient and could relay a message from capital to coast in minutes. The Harting Beacon station later utilised semaphore until the mid-nineteenth century, when the railways, with their own semaphore system, finally put paid to hill-to-hill signalling.

Now on the trig point there is one of those 'what you can see from here' plaques – lines all radiating from the centre (where you are) to prominent landmarks or towns. One of these, to the north-east, is Black Down – the up-line next signal station – but a wall of pines or conifers on the scarp line annoyingly obscures the view. Like Moses and the Red Sea, we wish we could part them temporarily just a little to get a sight line to Black Down. But we have used up our miracle quota for today by diverting the jet stream. Walk a little further down to the east, however, and you will get a peep around the end of the trees. And there it is: the unmistakeable southern promontory of the highest hill in the South Downs National Park. While you are down there, look across to the western slopes of the next hill. You should see a series of parallel lines – cross-dykes again – with the white snake of the South Downs Way cutting up and through them. The successive brows of the South Downs scarp retreat formation-like into the distance.

So Harting Beacon is bracketed by multiple cross-dykes on either side. I don't think that is accidental. I suspect that some 3,000 years ago Beacon Hill must have been a special place, a locality for a lot of significant community rituals, rather than a place of ordinary domestic settlement. Make your way southwards along the way parallel to the eastern side of the hill fort. Go straight on past its south-eastern corner, noting its prominent boundary bank running westwards across the top of the hill. Somewhere around here we spied a moth on a thistle, black on pink – not hard to spot. Later we found out that it was a five-spot burnet and the thistle a nodding one. On down the track, southwards, sun high in the sky, light streaming from the west. There is a convenient south-west-facing gate, with a little give in it for our backs. Not wanting to face Bertrand Russell on an empty stomach we stop to eat, wondering if Bertie had anything philosophical to say about picnics.

Replenished, actually rather too much replenished, we stroll on southwards, past the overgrown corner of a field where another barrow may lurk, through a small wood, and soon notice a complex of buildings on our right, screened by trees and bushes. Continue along the path to the end of the buildings, where copper beeches appear leading southwards at the top of the drive. The buildings are known as Telegraph House, home to Bertrand and Dora Russell's school from 1927. Here Bertie put to test his ideas on education, especially 'that men are born ignorant, not stupid; they are made stupid by education'. The school took in young boys and girls, for a modest fee, and fostered in them appreciation of science and modern humanities; classics were kept to a minimum. Knowledge was to be acquired not as an end in itself, but as a means to make a better world. The atmosphere was strikingly liberal for the day; free speech was actively encouraged, as was physical recreation. Vitality in all senses was stimulated and the strictures of traditional respectability were to be undone and cast aside.

Although the house is now privately owned, and sheltered from the footpaths, you can still glimpse the yellow-stuccoed tower at the south end, with its central oculus window. Bertie's study was in the top room and we can imagine him writing industriously on international affairs. Surrounded by an extensive library, a marble bust of Voltaire, numerous Chinese bronzes and ivories, and his brother's old brass telescope, he could inspect the view from Leith Hill and Hindhead to the sea and the Isle of Wight. Of this room Russell was later to write that he had never seen one with a more beautiful view. Not all his writing was so cerebral; he often had to draft letters to forgetful parents who had omitted to pay the school fees.

We retreat, unusually pensive, trying to assess how much damage our education has done, back through the woods, striking a path – again on the South Downs Way – north-west along the edge of Little Round Down. Turn left off the way a few hundred metres further on, and saunter down a pleasant green trackway, a forest of foxgloves to our right. It is much quieter here. Towards the bottom of the path there is a second fenced ring, and on closer inspection we find that it encloses a dew pond which holds a little water. We are unsure why these have been fenced off. Are we dealing with some extreme application of health and safety legisla-

tion? Are dew ponds now dangerous? We hope not. At this place the eye is inevitably drawn to a beguiling green path that inclines upwards along a dry valley to the north-west, a dense sloping hanger of trees to its left, the path disappearing in mid-distance to the right. Painters exploit this technique which must trigger some deeply ingrained inclination to explore. We follow our instincts and take the path.

Bertrand Russell's study lies at the top of this tower, the window hidden by foliage. With its panoramic views, it must have been a pleasant retreat from the hurly-burly of the school.

A monumental folly? The Vandalia Tower once housed a banqueting room with views to die for.

It is wonderfully peaceful – a serene green stroll – the silence broken only by occasional birdsong and, at one point, the collective buzz of a bee swarm. Soon we climb, with some regret, back on to the heights of Harting Down and re-join the South Downs Way, heading westwards back to the car park. The runners have long since run on and the puddles have mostly dried out. But we have one more destination to reach. On through the car park, across the road, we follow the South Downs Way down into woods a short distance. Leaving the path, we scramble up to reach the skyline. We think you will see, to your right, the ruins of the tower you saw at the start of your walk. Don't cross the fence as the tower is on private land, but this is the Vandalia Tower, and this is where the West Virginia bit comes in.

It was built probably in 1773 by the owner of Uppark House, Sir Matthew Fetherstonehaugh, to celebrate his investment in a new unofficial colony on the Ohio River, known as Vandalia. The tower functioned as a magnificent banqueting or viewing house. The viewing room was on the upper floor, with kitchens beneath. Built of brick and stone, surviving illustrations demonstrate that it was a fairy-tale confection of Gothic windows, castellated turrets and spires. Some of you, I am sure, have some acquaintance with Cinderella's castle at Disney World. Well, it wasn't as big as that, but it was just as anomalous, just as jaw-dropping.

Unfortunately, this fairy tale did not have a happy ending. The American Revolution put paid to Vandalia, and a fire destroyed most of the tower in 1842. Bertie was no supporter of colonialism. I imagine him here, surrounded by children, using the ruined folly as a material metaphor for demonstrating the injustice of taking another people's land by force. Lecture over, he lets them off the leash, telling them to choose whatever route they want back to Telegraph House.

SOFA STATS

The starting point for this walk is the small car park east of the B2141 at the top of the hill (roughly SU 790 180). The total length of walk is approximately 7.5km (4.5 miles). The elevation range is from 129m to 234m above sea level. Minimum walking time is two hours.

ONE ARTICLE TO LOOK AT BEFORE YOU GO

Bruneau, William (2003), 'New Evidence on Life, Learning and Medical Care at Beacon Hill School', *Russell: the Journal of Bertrand Russell Studies*, Vol. 23, Iss. 2, Article 13. Available at http://digitalcommons.mcmaster.ca/russelljournal/vol23/iss2/13.

WALK 11: JUNE

BLACK DOWN – THE TEMPLE OF THE WINDS

IN A NUTSHELL

Black Down is an imposing sandstone hill at the western end of the Weald and in the northern part of the South Downs National Park. It is the highest point in Sussex at 280m and the sweeping views from its flanks and southern promontory are truly memorable. Unsurprisingly, it can be also viewed from afar, especially from the chalk hills to the south. For those people who care to look, therefore, it can be an unwavering presence, a constant rather brooding reminder. The archaeology of Black Down is not dramatically obvious – there are no great hill forts

Tree-covered and brooding, Black Down lies in the north of the Park. The Temple of the Winds is at its southern tip (left) while Aldworth lies at its northern end.

or medieval castles. But there are prehistoric flint tools, subtle Bronze Age earth-works, trackways, a telegraph station and the discreetly concealed house of the Victorian Age's most honoured poet – Alfred Lord Tennyson. And there are also benches, one grand, the others more homely, dedicated to the memories of people who loved Black Down.

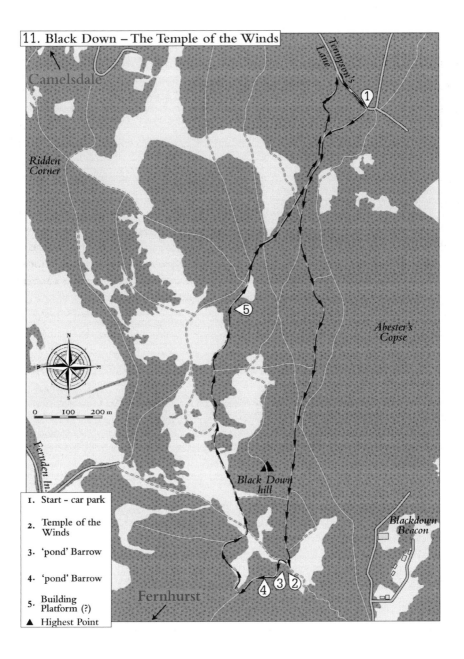

11. Black Down – The Temple of the Winds

1. Start - car park

2. Temple of the Winds

3. 'pond' Barrow

4. 'pond' Barrow

5. Building Platform (?)

▲ Highest Point

TIME TO GET GOING

The best place to start is to drive or walk up Tennyson's Lane, and commence your walk from the more easterly car park at SU 922 306. Our navigational advice is to appreciate that there is a relatively flat-topped hill stretching southwards from you, with steep sides to the east and west. Keep to the eastern scarp on your way out and the western scarp (at least for the first section) on your return. Go through the wooden five-bar gate and keep to the left to reach quickly your first view at Robin's bench. No wonder he liked it here. There are spectacular views to the south-east, where, in the distance on top of the chalk ridge, you can make out the clump of trees on Chanctonbury Ring. But even more impressive are the rolling greensand hills closer to you, but geologically older than the chalk behind them. Sitting on Robin's bench, one side of the vista is framed by a young Scots pine, that national tree of Scotland and characteristic of the tree cover on Black Down. The other dominant tree on the hill is beech.

A little further on brings you to a bench shared by Stephen and Carys. I liked it that they were memorialised side by side, and each had a small inscription. One told of the power of love to conquer mortality, the other invited us to admire the view and become an acquaintance. The spectacle was indeed a serene, easterly one across the Weald and into infinity. Bidding them farewell, follow the paths to where they fork, taking the left tine. Now this is where you have to keep looking at the sandy ground beneath your feet. At various times during the twentieth

Robin's bench on Black Down. Warmed in the sun, it affords a sweeping perspective south-east towards the chalk Downs.

century, but particularly during excavations in 1903–04, a large number of flint tools were found on this part of the hill. Most date to the late Mesolithic period and therefore are about 7,000 years old; they would have been used by people who relied on hunting, gathering and fishing for their livelihoods. The implements comprise arrowheads, scrapers, hammerstones, a perforated macehead, axes and plenty of tiny flints known as microliths.

Now there are at least two things that are interesting about these finds. The first is the raw material. Most implements were of flint, which must have come from the chalk lands of the North or South Downs, implying that bands of hunters could have travelled to Black Down from those areas. The second curious thing is to wonder why hunters and gatherers at that time (and remember there must have been very few of them) came to Black Down in the first place. It is hard to believe that there were food resources special to Black Down. We are sure the local bilberries were delicious but equally confident that they could have been found closer to home. Some may argue that Black Down was high and dry, and therefore provided a good trackway around the western end of the Weald for roving bands of hunter-gatherers. But that is a rather catch-all explanation. So here is the hunch. I think Black Down was recognised as a special place some 7,000 years ago, perhaps not for the same reasons as today, but still exotic, apart from daily life, mysterious, sacred even.

As you walk on southwards, and as soon as you get tired of looking for flints, heads up and look around. The landscape is a mixture of heather, gorse, foxgloves, beech and pine. In more recent centuries commoners used to graze their livestock on Black Down, and no doubt collect plant material for bedding and wood for fuel. Their activities kept the tree and scrub cover under control, and allowed the heather, and its associated fauna, space to grow. Nowadays the commoners are no more and the landscape has to be managed to ensure that the heather is not crowded out. So don't be surprised if you spot a few grazing black cows; they are keeping the scrub down. I liked their unfenced roaming, emerging unexpectedly from the undergrowth, munching purposively and pensively. They are conservationists, after all.

Keep striding south. Soon you will note, especially on your right, the very hummocky and uneven nature of the ground, carpeted with beech mast and fallen leaves. The surface is anything but flat, rather giving the appearance of being much dug over. It is quite likely that chert was quarried here in the nineteenth century for road stone, and perhaps there was some sand-digging as well. If there were earlier archaeological earthworks here, they are now going to be difficult to identify. Round barrows are so ubiquitous in other areas of the South Downs National Park, including its heathlands, and we have seen so many, so we are programmed to seek them out. But, if they exist here, they are lying low. Much more obvious are the small ponds whose still waters reflect the verticals of the Scots pines towering over them. There is a story that the name, Black Down, comes from the dark and heathery nature of the hill. It probably was a deserted place of darkness in the past, with no fires from settlements relieving its moon-lit slumber. But downs in this part of the world are associated with either the white of chalk or the green of turf. So lending the colour of black to a down makes it distinctive. Gazing down into the waters of those peaty ponds, you wonder if the name is not a reflection of these black mirrors. Time to let your hair blow. Let's go to the Temple of the Winds.

The Temple of the Winds★ is a very atmospheric and, I am sure at times, windy place. Black Down was a favoured location in the Victorian period for walkers and naturalists, writers and artists. And it may be at that time that this southern-most point of Black Down was christened with such an evocative moniker. The original Temple of the Winds was an octagonal tower in the Roman forum at Athens, on which a weather vane in the form of Triton indicated the direction of the wind. Here there is no tower or Triton, but a much more useful and elegant curved stone bench. Edward Hunter installed this in memory of his wife Mabel when he gave Black Down to the National Trust in 1944. Now it is the perfect spot for our sandwiches, while, aided by the orientation plaque in front of us, we argue about the identifications of the various summits along the chalk ridge to the south-east, in the distance.

A small promontory to the south-east of this part of the hill was used as a sig-nalling station at various times in the past. Some claim that news of the Spanish Armada in the Channel in July 1588 was relayed by a chain of fire beacons (one of

The curved seat at the Temple of the Winds which records the donation of Black Down to the National Trust by Edward Hunter.

them on Black Down) to London. Certainly such a beacon was here by the end of the seventeenth century. At the end of the following century, from 1796 to 1816, signalling technology had become less of a fire risk, and a shutter chain station was established here to convey messages from the Admiralty in London to the fleet at Portsmouth. Basically messages were signalled through the differing positions of six large octagonal shutters on small towers. The next station southwards was Beacon Hill on Harting Down, and northwards, Hascombe, in Surrey. Adjacent to the towers were small huts, no doubt containing the personnel who would ferry messages up and down the line.

Much more curious, and potentially a lot older, is a smallish circular earthwork about 17m in diameter just up slope and behind the Temple of the Winds. You can make out the remains of curving banks, about 0.5m high, that enclose a circular space. The significance of this earthwork was a matter of inconclusive debate, but a recent discovery of a second very similarly sized enclosure to the west of the known one suggests a possible explanation. The fact that there are two of these enclosures suggests that they might be prehistoric burial, or more likely ceremonial, monuments dating from the Bronze Age, known as 'pond barrows'. As the name suggests, they are not barrow mounds at all but rather flat, sometimes slightly dished areas, surrounded by a small bank and ditch. So walk down a little to the west and see if you can find the second pond barrow. It is roughly at SU 918 292 on slightly sloping ground, and just to the south of the track; it lies in a semi-open clearing covered with fallen beech leaves and a few ferns.

Now trees are all very well and we love them to bits, and they are the lungs of the planet and so on, but just occasionally you wish that they wouldn't crowd together so often. Sometimes they get in the way. We resolve to come back in the winter when there is less of a leaf canopy. It is difficult to see the nearest range of chalk downs to the south, which includes Harting Down. There are a great number of prehistoric barrows on the chalk, but very few pond barrows. I suspect that a view southwards was as important to pond-barrow builders as it was to eighteenth-century signallers, and vice versa. Black Down was exceptional then and now; because of its location, geology and vegetation it was a reclusive place, out of the ordinary. Special place, special barrows.

Turn northwards back along the spine of Black Down. You soon pass Colin's bench, which is in need of a little tlc, and you can then enjoy the big-sky views to the west towards Selborne and Butser Hill, south of Petersfield. There are fewer trees on this western side and the cattle have done a good job, allowing the heather to flourish. The next bench plate tells us that Sheena and her dog, Sam, used to love walking here. We can imagine Sam darting between the clumps of heather, disappearing and suddenly reappearing, intent on pursuit but keeping a watchful eye on Sheena. The paths here are occasionally worn so that you can see irregular, but flat, buff-coloured sandstone slabs forming a natural mosaic and pavement. The seats and names now come thick and fast: Mrs Whitton (slightly formal) but then families, Harold, May and their daughter Hazel. These memorials should be sad but instead they are rather joyous, and we feel we can appreciate something that they too loved.

Soon you come to a place where multiple paths intersect, so bear to the right taking a track that will lead back to the western-most car park. Somewhere around here, a little to the east of the track, masked by fern, gorse and a holly bush, is what appears to be a rectangular platform – the sort of thing where a hut might once have stood. It's roughly at SU 918 300. Is this the place where the occasional com-moner used to sleep, anxious to keep an eye on sleeping cattle, or is it the location for a small late Victorian arbour, the sort of place where Tennyson would himself would have sat, in isolated contemplation, as far from the madding crowd as the south-east of England permitted?

We hurry on past more ponds, smiling sympathetically at a straggly group of walkers being frog-marched towards a line of Scots pine on the western skyline, then along our last sandy paths, eventually reaching the National Trust interpreta-tion board. Here we read of the Trust's attempts to clear Black Down of invasive rhododendron (which we applaud) and wish that such clearance would also include the horrible white-painted pyramid that is designed to collect donations and car park charges. Out on to Tennyson Lane, with care, and then back to the south-east to reach our originating car park – right opposite a driveway that bears the name of Aldworth beside it. And there hangs a tale. Or rather poem.

At the end of that disappearing drive, hidden from view, lies the neo-Gothic-styled Aldworth House, home to Alfred Lord Tennyson from 1869 until his death in 1892. Tennyson's poetry was greatly admired by Queen Victoria and he held the post of Poet Laureate from the 1850s until his death. His most famous work is perhaps *The Charge of the Light Brigade*, a dramatic tribute to the British cavalrymen involved in an ill-advised charge on 25 October 1854, during the Crimean War. Tennyson was much involved in the design of Aldworth, and patriotically had the foundation stone laid on Shakespeare's birth-day, 23 April 1868. He moved to Black Down in July 1869 from the Isle of Wight in order to

Aldworth – this drive leads to the former home of England's longest serving poet laureate – Alfred Lord Tennyson. But it is private property and still hidden from view.

WALK 11

escape the attention of tourists. He was, after all, a victim of Victorian celebrity culture. He chose well in Black Down. The house remains largely hidden from view, both from far and near.

I think Tennyson got Black Down right. It is, and was, a place removed from the everyday. A hill where you could sit, stroll and think, mind cleared of the clutter of everyday. It is still one of the best places in the South Downs National Park to observe the star-filled night sky. The intrinsic other-worldliness of Black Down was recognised and no doubt revered by bands of hunters 7,000 years ago, by worshippers at those earthwork circles some 3,500 years ago, and by countless unnamed through the ages who have left no record of their visits and thoughts. Black Down was a dearly thoughtful place for Robin, Stephen, Carys, Edward, Mabel, Colin, Mrs Whitton, Harold, May and Hazel – not forgetting Sheena and her dog Sam. We imagine also for Alfred. Let's leave him walking those same paths we have just trodden, shabby cloak drawn tight, wideawake★★ firmly fixed. At night, his way lit by lantern or stars, the wind swirling beech leaves around his feet, a nightjar looking for a mate churring in the distance, tall Scots Pines creaking overhead. Drama enough you would think. But his thoughts are elsewhere, alive with tales of King Arthur, the Knights, their Round Table.

SOFA STATS

Begin the walk at the eastern most car park at approximately SU 922 306. The total length of walk is approximately 3 miles (5 kilometres). The elevation range is from 236 metres to 280 metres above sea-level. Minimum walking time is 2 hours.

ONE BOOK TO LOOK AT BEFORE YOU GO

Tennyson at Aldworth: *The Diary of James Henry Mangles* by James H Mangles and Earl A Knies (1984). Ohio: Ohio University Press.

★ Not to be confused with *The Temple of the Four Winds* on nearby Hurt Hill, Hindhead – also owned by the National Trust.

★★ A wideawake hat was formed from soft felt and had a broad rim and low crown. Tennyson was so attached to his that Prime Minister Gladstone worried that the only difficulty in offering him a peerage was that he might insist on wearing it in the House of Lords.

WALK 12: JUNE

PETERSFIELD – THE TOWN BY THE LAKE

IN A NUTSHELL

The extraordinary thing about Petersfield is its ordinariness. It is a small market town in the Hampshire section of the South Downs National Park. It doesn't have a stand-out building like the cathedrals of Winchester or Chichester, or the great houses of Cowdray or Petworth, or the castles of Arundel or Lewes. No major rivers flow alongside or through it. It does have a collection of medieval and later houses, but also has its fair share of 1960s intrusions. No one especially famous lived in the town and left their legacy there. Happily situated on the route between London and Portsmouth, it was a popular staging post in the past, significant now for the people who once sought brief hospitality there. Daniel Defoe, writing of his tour through Britain in 1726, remarked: 'Petersfield … a town prominent for little but it being full of good inns.' The perceived nondescript character of the place informs modern historians. A booklet by the local historical society on the town concludes: 'Nobody famous was born, lived or died here. Nothing very special happened here. All the famous people just stopped here on their way to somewhere else.' It is even claimed that there is no Morris dancing in the town. Dull or what? Why would you want to walk around it? To find out you need to read on.

TIME TO GET GOING

Let's start at the obvious place – the market square (unsurprisingly known as the Square), right in the centre of the town (SU 746 232). Bordering the south side of the Square is the church of St Peter's, a twelfth-century foundation by the

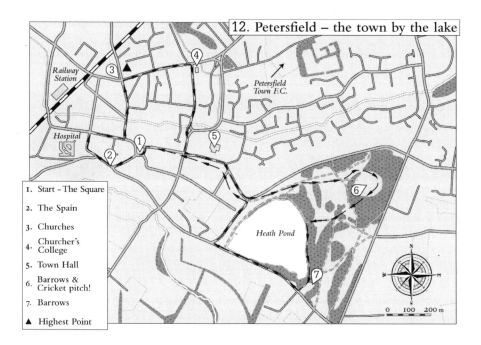

12. Petersfield – the town by the lake

Railway Station

Petersfield Town F.C.

Hospital

Heath Pond

1. Start - The Square
2. The Spain
3. Churches
4. Churcher's College
5. Town Hall
6. Barrows & Cricket pitch!
7. Barrows
▲ Highest Point

0   100   200 m

Earl of Gloucester, a son of Henry I. He wanted to develop a market on a sandy ridge between two streams, but at the crossing of some important trade routes. By 1184 the emerging town had a charter, with the church, square and high street to the east forming the kernel of the settlement. The striking centrepiece of the church interior is the twelfth-century chancel with its central semi-circular dog-toothed arch and the three round-headed windows above.

Outside, and dominating the centre of the Square, is the statue of a horsed William III, apparently in the guise of Roman Emperor Marcus Aurelius, mounted on a plinth. His classical resemblance comes from his lack of stirrups and an alleged Roman nose. William III was the Protestant King of England from 1689, and popular for taking part in several wars against the Catholic King of France, Louis XIV. But this statue was not intended to adorn the Square. It once stood in the grounds of Petersfield House, owned by the prominent Joliffe family who paid for the statue. However, the house was demolished in 1793, and the statue moved to its current location. To be frank, we don't like it – it looks out of place, which, of course, it is. To the right of the church is a brick-built three-storey structure whose eighteenth-century façade hides a timber-framed medieval building. There is a helpful blue plaque on the wall (there are a number of these in the town) which tells you that the premises was once owned by Richard Churcher in the 1690s (who founded Churcher's College) and in 1802 by John Small, maker of cricket balls and one of the best batsmen in England. We will meet both the college and cricket again.

PETERSFIELD

William III, in the guise of Roman Emperor Marcus Aurelius, dominates the market square at Petersfield.

No. 18 Sheep Street. The upper courses of the façade have been covered with mathematical tiles, while the ground floor courses are in brick. It's quite easy to overlook the difference.

Walk down Sheep Street, which derived its name from the importance of the sheep trade to the town. There are some colourful timber-framed and jettied buildings on its south side. Look out for Nos 18 and 20. These were originally one property of the Wealden Hall type, with a central hearth open to the ceiling, but have now been divided into two homes. Have a good look at the upper storey of No. 18, faced with mathematical tiles which resemble bricks. They are a good imitation, and even close up it's difficult to spot the difference. These 'bricks' are an architectural tax avoidance device, since there was a tax on real bricks between 1784 and 1850. At this point, dear reader, permit yourself a sigh. Often life just seems to be a series of struggles between taxes and how to escape them, legally of course. The government soon put an end to this architectural sleight of hand by imposing a tax on tiles.

A much more interesting open grassed space lies at the end of Sheep Street, called the Spain. It is also very pleasant, completely free of misplaced statuary, but fringed with fine houses. Uncertainty surrounds the origin of the name. There is a suggestion that it may refer to weaned or 'spained' lambs. On the other hand *spann* is an Old Norse word for tiles and so could refer to the tiled roofs of nearby properties, but we are unsure whether the Vikings got as far inland as Petersfield – we think, on reflection, probably not. Much the most attractive, if unlikely, hypothesis is that the name derives from seasonal influxes of Spanish wool merchants, presumably intent on acquiring Hampshire fleece. Imagining the social mingling of a group of Spanish *comerciantes de lana* with the locals of Petersfield – well, that could have been an eye-opener. But you will have to remain contented with one unassailable fact: the gabled brick-fronted house on the west side of the Spain, the one with the semi-circular windows on the topmost storey, once belonged to the great botanist John Goodyer (1592–1664), 'the ablest Herbalist now living in England'. He introduced the Jerusalem artichoke to England. It is a misnomer, as it has no relation to Jerusalem and is not an artichoke. And do heed Goodyer's warning: 'which way so ever they be dressed and eaten, they stir and cause a filthy loathsome stinking wind within the body, thereby causing the belly to be pained and tormented, and are a meat more fit for swine than men.'

Exit the Spain to the north-west, noting the tile-hung and buttressed building as you approach Swan Street, which dates from 1579 and whose occupants included a well-known composer of hymns. The side of the building reveals some of the timber-framed elements that indicate its early date. On the corner of Swan Street and Chapel Street, take a look at the timber-framed and jettied upper storey of a sixteenth-century farmhouse. Flora Twort, a local artist, once had a studio here. Walking up Chapel Street, there is much to remark. We were much impressed with the alternating cream-and-red brickwork of the arched windows on the west side of the street. Further on there is an eighteenth-century inn. A frequent guest was H.G. Wells, who often dined and wrote in its rooms; he spent his early years at nearby Uppark House. A little further it is easy to miss the canalised Drum stream, before you come up fast against the Methodist church on Station Road.

The ivy-clad eighteenth-century Churcher's College. Archaeologist Stuart Piggott was one of its most famous former pupils.

The population of Petersfield did not want for choice of religion. The Methodist church, built of flint, cornered with brick buttresses and small towers and crowned by a spire, was erected around the start of the twentieth century. Directly opposite it, and architecturally in opposition, is the Catholic church dedicated to St Laurence, built by the Cave family at roughly the same time. The church of St Laurence, on a sunny Sunday afternoon, looked like a vision from some Italian hilltop town. These two buildings could not be more unlike. But as we wandered eastwards down Station Road, a quick backwards glance told us that, in the location stakes, there was only one winner. The Methodist building dominates the perspective and occupants leaving their Victorian and Edwardian homes in this stretch of town must have found its façade, and calling, difficult to ignore.

Soon you turn southwards down College Street and on your left, ivy clad, is the geometric façade of the eponymous Churcher's College. The little blue plaque records that in the eighteenth century Richard Churcher left money to build a school so that young boys could be instructed in mathematics and navigation for apprenticeship to the East India Company. The school moved to a new site in 1881 and the building is now occupied by Hampshire County Council. The rather squat brick building on the other side of the road is the oldest surviving (late fourteenth century) domestic structure in the town. The brick frontage, cloaking the timber frame, was added to the building in the eighteenth century. The blind window is, of course, a tax avoidance device to escape the window tax, which was repealed in 1851. Stride on past the United Reform church (formerly the old Congregational church), the whitewashed and timber-framed pub called The Good Intent, a sixteenth-century coaching inn, and definitely past The White Hart, a boarded-up victim of austerity. Turn left down Heath Road. At the end of this road are things that make Petersfield really exceptional, not only the combination of heath and lake which have provided generations of Petersfielders with the space to row, play, fish and ramble, but also an extraordinary collection of prehistoric burial mounds.

While ambling down Heath Road glance to the left and see the rather incongruous town hall, erected in 1936 in art deco style. And just before you get to the lake note the large late Victorian or Edwardian tile-hung houses, built to take advantage of the heathland views to the east. This large expanse of open ground on the edge of Petersfield was used by the medieval town dwellers as common land on which their cattle could be grazed, and no doubt its other natural resources, such as timber and heather, were frequently exploited. By the eighteenth century part of it had become so boggy that animals sometimes drowned in it. In 1735 some citizens got together to dredge the bog and built an earthen bank around it, creating the pond. It soon became an area used for leisure. By 1775 there was a bowling green and tennis courts. It was also a popular place for fishing. Such was its popularity that by 1820 the heath had become home to what became popularly called the Taro Fair, for trading sheep and cattle. Taro was a corruption of the Welsh word for bull (*taru*), so we can imagine an annual influx of Welsh-speaking drovers in the town's inns. Not quite as exotic as the fabled Iberian wool merchants, but a welcome diversion for some of the townsfolk.

Once you are lakeside, walk around it in a clockwise direction, heading for the north-east corner of the heath. The cricket pitch should be easy to find; it was moved to the Heath in 1858. When you have admired the quality of the turf, and even applauded the local batsmen if there is a match on, you will notice

Sunday cricket near the lake at Petersfield. On the far side lies a large, grass-covered Bronze Age burial mound, one of twenty-one such monuments in the vicinity.

some large mounds around the perimeter, suspiciously all just outside the pitch's boundary. These are Bronze Age burial mounds, probably thrown up around some 3,500 years ago, some of which at least will cover the dead of local communities – inhumations or cremations. Walk all around the boundary and you should be able to climb on at least four or five such barrows. From the top of some of them you can even get a good view of the cricket. They make excellent, if a little irreverent, places on which to down your cheese sandwiches. But we wonder about the cricket pitch, and can't help thinking that sometime in the past one or two barrows were flattened to make way for it.

Between the pitch and the north-eastern corner of the heath, there are a few other barrows, some covered by ferns and foxgloves. Leaving the match behind, stride southwards a little and then westwards towards the lake – you should come across another cluster of barrows. Some of them seem to have been deliberately planted with rings of pine trees in the much more recent past. No doubt such plantings were done with every good intention but it may well be that the interference from tree roots plays havoc with the archaeological layers within the barrows. Overall there are at least twenty-one barrows, probably of distinct forms, in this part of the heath, all east of the lake. I think it is quite likely that there were more, and while it is difficult to be absolutely sure, this seems to be the largest barrow cemetery in the South Downs National Park. Surprisingly, none of the barrows seems to have been excavated in modern times.

Continue your walk around the south side of the lake and you eventually come to an interpretation board that has a plan of the barrows. A cursory examination of the plan suggests that some of the barrows could be in lines, some of which could have been aligned on sunsets. It is tempting to wonder whether an earlier, boggy, version of the current pond existed some 3,500 years ago. Perhaps offerings were thrown into the water to appease the spirits of the dead. Maybe those workers who created the pond in the eighteenth century found the odd artefact. If they did, they kept things to themselves.

Make your way back to town along Heath Road, eventually coming to the High Street. Wandering down the High Street, past the war memorial, will take you back to the Square, but there are some interesting buildings (and blue plaques to read) on the way. Walled burgage plots survive either side of the street and a physic garden is laid out in one of the plots, behind No. 16. The porticoed and geometric façade of Winton House was once part of the White Hart Inn, bordering the original coaching road between Portsmouth and London. Samuel Pepys, secretary of the navy, often stayed here, his gradually deteriorating eyesight presumably not hindering his eye for the ladies. Bath Travel Agents now occupy a sixteenth-century building that housed popular tearooms, known as Punch and Judy, from the 1930s onwards. A partial survival of a building of similar date is No. 6 High Street. And if you are a sentimentalists, like us, do pop into the Rams Walk arcade and say a kind word to the shepherd and his dog, who looks bewildered, as well he might, sat sandwiched between a newsagent and a supermarket.

WALK 12

Let's get back to the Square. You deserve a drink. There are plenty of types on offer. While you sip or sup, quaff or quench, we want to leave you some last thoughts.

Petersfield as a town is perhaps unexceptional, especially when compared with the numerous historic towns that populate southern England. And indeed, some things in it seem out of place: William III, the town hall and the sad shepherd. But its very ordinariness is something to celebrate. We can concentrate on the historically typical and usual without the distractions caused by the presence of the Great and the Good. It's a local town for local people, who in the 1820s played no small part in improving democracy in England, appealing against the then Lord of the Manor's chosen stooges for Members of Parliament. Even the well-known local painter Flora Twort, who exhibited in London, painted scenes of ordinary Petersfielders going about their ordinary daily lives, whether in the Square on market days or on the Heath.

The headline-making days of Petersfield may be yet to come. And it may be down to archaeology. A very influential archaeologist, Stuart Piggott, attended Churcher's College in the 1920s, and his first archaeological essay, written in a school notebook, was 'The Prehistoric Remains at Petersfield'. The manuscript survives in Oxford. Such is Piggott's importance that he surely merits a local blue plaque somewhere in the town. At least he has been memorialised in a new housing development – a group of upmarket houses in Piggott Place, north of the Heath. But that is an aside. If an organised exploration of the barrows at Petersfield gets under way (and at the time of writing that seems a possibility), I feel quietly confident that something remarkable will be discovered. The Bronze Age chiefs of prehistoric Petersfield may yet reveal themselves to an awestruck global audience who might clog the Heath and High Street to pay their respects.

SOFA STATS

Begin your walk at the Square, in the centre of town (SU 746 232). The total length of walk is approximately 4.5km (3 miles). The elevation range is from 55m to 66m above sea level. Minimum walking time is two and a half hours.

ONE OR TWO BOOKS TO LOOK AT BEFORE YOU GO

Leaton, E. *et al.* (1996), *A Petersfield Perambulation*. Petersfield: Petersfield Area Historical Society. Available from the Tourist Information Centre in the Square, along with *The Blue Plaque Trail*.

Hick, K. (2005), *Petersfield: A History & Celebration*. Salisbury: The Francis Frith Collection.

UP AND DOWN OLD WINCHESTER HILL

IN A NUTSHELL

This is a walk that will take you from valley to down; to be precise, from the clear waters of the river Meon, to the summit of Old Winchester Hill. There are pleasant villages in the valley – places like Exton, Meonstoke and Corhampton straddling the Meon, with their ancient churches. And there is a walk up to Old Winchester Hill with its prehistoric barrows and later Iron Age hill fort. The question to ponder as you wind your way along and upwards is the relationship between the two – between down and valley. I suspect there always has been one. The waters of the Meon are crystal clear, gently susurrant and flowing over emerald-green vegetation that trails in the direction of the flow. The river is so clean because it rises in the chalk south of East Meon, unlike the rivers further to the east that have their watershed in the clayey Weald.

TIME TO GET GOING

Let's start from what looks like an unofficial car park just to the west of the A32 and north of Exton – it's where the South Downs Way crosses the main road. There is space there for a few cars (SU 617 212). Cross the road carefully and join the South Downs Way and traverse the Meon by means of a small wooden bridge. You get a good view down into the water here. Then head towards Shavards Farm and stride broadly eastwards towards Old Winchester Hill. The farm is important in terms of location because it was near here that both an exceptionally well-preserved façade of an agricultural building of the Roman period was excavated and some early Saxon burials, associated with a settlement of sunken huts. We can

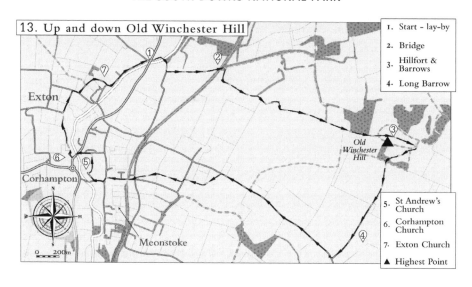

13. Up and down Old Winchester Hill	1. Start - lay-by
	2. Bridge
	3. Hillfort & Barrows
	4. Long Barrow
	5. St Andrew's Church
	6. Corhampton Church
	7. Exton Church
	▲ Highest Point

Half overgrown, you come upon the brick bridge supporting a disused railway that once linked Alton and Fareham quite suddenly. If you didn't know this, it would appear like a rather grand entrance.

be confident, therefore, that intensive agricultural exploitation of the valley was under way at least by the Roman period, and I suspect a good deal earlier.

Follow the South Downs Way along a path lined in part with coppiced hazel. We spent our time looking for nuts, but only found one. Pleasantly lost in this timeless task, and surrounded by branches and birdsong, it was a great shock to be confronted suddenly by a large, tree-shrouded brick-built structure with what looked like a doorless gateway through it. It was such a shock, in fact, that it momentarily rewired my perceptions and for all the world I felt like I had somehow been transported to stand outside the entrance of some old British colonial fort. It may have been wishful thinking but I felt the humidity levels soar and didn't I catch a glimpse of what looked like a monkey on the parapet? Probably nanoseconds later, order was restored, and we realised that we stood in front of a bridge that once carried the railway between Alton and Fareham. This line was authorised by Act of Parliament in 1896 and opened in 1903, making it one of the last railways in the UK constructed to mainline standards. It was closed to passenger traffic in 1955 and to freight in 1961. As a boy who grew up intoxicated by the smoke from steam trains leaving Temple Meads station, I will always have a soft spot for such things. I want to sit on the bridge parapet with my gran and wait for the train, its rhythmical chugging announcing its presence long before it whistles into view. The humidity must be getting to me. Anyway, now it's known as the Meon Valley Trail and Bridleway. Onwards and upwards – the call of Old Winchester Hill will not be denied.

Follow the ascending South Downs Way by the sides of fields towards the woodland belt that lies on the western slopes of the hill. The whole hill, as well as being rich in archaeological remains, is also an important nature reserve. The woods we walk through to reach the hill fort contain quite a lot of ash, but there are also stands of juniper and yew amongst the scrub, and the hill is home to a large butterfly population. Emerging from the woods, just past the five-bar gate, we come abruptly up against some Bronze Age barrows that have stood here for about 4,000 years, and were thrown up a long time before the hill fort was constructed.

Walk on through the western end of the fort, whose perimeter is defined by an impressive earthen bank and external ditch, and inside you quickly come across three large barrows, with apparently a 'saucer' or 'pond' barrow to the east of them. I admit to a slight hesitancy – hence the quotation marks. This particular saucer seems really quite deep. Geological events can cause holes in the chalk, such as phenomena known as sinkholes and dissolution pipes. But my geologist friend tells me it is none of these. Saucer or pond barrows are interesting, however, in that they seem to be the mirror image of mound barrows; when they are close together it seems like one has been formed from the other, which it may well have been. Stride on along the central spine of the fort towards and through the eastern gate, and then turn to the north to find Maggie's wooden bench (her name is inscribed on it) and a nearby interpretation board.

Realisations now come thick and fast. First, we check in our rucksack to discover that we have broken one of our golden rules – no cheese sandwiches! We have to make do with haggled shares of a chocolate bar. Second, who was Maggie? Not much to go on here, other than that she was loved a lot, and, like us, enjoyed Old Winchester Hill. Third, and this is where it gets a little more archaeological, we think the whole hill must have been one monumental barrow cemetery some

WALK 13

4,000 years ago. There are barrows inside and outside the hill fort, and barrows that the hill fort ditch-diggers dug through on the fort's southern side. There are at least thirteen barrows over the hilltop – and I imagine there are a good few more lying under the turf. The ones inside the hill fort are in a clear east–west line, making us think about alignments and celestial bodies, and were 'respected', i.e. not destroyed by the later hill-fort builders.

The interpretation board is informative and helpful, suggesting that the barrows would have initially been 'brilliant white markers on the skyline', which is true. However, to remain so would have involved active maintenance, weeding and general scrub clearance, perhaps by the relatives of the deceased or the followers of a dead chief. There is a little interpretative sleight of hand in the information provided on the board with respect to the hill fort. There is a lovely picture of twenty or so round-houses illustrated within the fort and it looks quite full and just how we imagine it ought to look. The problem is that this fort has never been excavated and geophysical surveys of the interior (magnetometry) undertaken in the 1990s by English Heritage only demonstrated thin scatters of pits interspersed with empty areas. The problem is, it is quite difficult generalising from one hill fort to another; no two hill forts, especially if they are adjacent, seem similarly used in the past. And the interpretation board is silent on what our Bronze Age mourners or Iron Age hill-fort builders thought of the butterflies. They would have had a view, I am sure of it. Now if you have time you can wander further along the ridge to the north-east. Fine views back to the hill fort to be had. However, short of our cheese sandwiches, we decided to head southwards, down the contours, and along the footpath towards Stocks Cottage.

Rather denuded by sheep scrapes, the long barrow below Old Winchester Hill looks forlornly shorn.

Passing those buildings, you will notice quite a modern-looking brick-surrounded well. I peered down to check out the water, some distance down. It made my memory smile. I once heard a talk about hill forts by one of those fast-disappearing old colonial types. At the end of the lecture – silence – until someone rather timorously asked: 'and where did they get their water from?' (Usually in hill forts there are no wells or indeed clay-lined ponds – remember chalk is porous). 'They sent the women out every morning with empty pots,' thundered the reply. I can't help feeling that there was some truth in this: women processing down the forerunner of the South Downs Way filling their pots with Meon water. Must have been hard going back up though.

Just past Stocks Cottage you come up alongside a restored shepherd's hut, flint-walled and brick-cornered, one room, a fireplace and a beaten earth floor. Weak lambs, or those whose mothers had died, would be brought into the warmth here. And to the east, on the far side of the field, stands a rather eroded and scruffy-looking long mound. Now actually this is the oldest monument on our walk – a long barrow from the Neolithic period, perhaps some 5,500 years old. The barrow was originally surrounded by a bank and ditch. 'Excavations' in the early 1800s apparently uncovered an adult skeleton and a silver coin. Such an association rules out a prehistoric date, so taken at face value, this burial might have been Roman or later, but definitely a long time after the barrow was constructed. Whoever was buried in the long barrow in the first instance, and quite possibly it was more than one individual, would have been among the first generation of farmers in the Meon valley. Their cattle, sheep and crops grew and grazed in fields between the barrow and the river. As you take your leave, a glance backwards frames the hill fort and the shepherd's hut. You can't help but notice a large 'M' in tile on the roof of the latter. Who was this 'M'? Is this our Maggie?

You are at an interesting point in the landscape, particularly in relation to the ages of the fields that surround you. To the east, uphill, are large fields with straight boundaries. These date from the eighteenth- and nineteenth-century enclosure of common land. In the medieval period this was all open grazing land. To the west, between you and the modern villages, was a 'ladder system' of small, rectangular fields strung either side of Stocks Lane. Air photographic evidence demonstrates that an even earlier, prehistoric complex of small rectangular fields on a different alignment underlies the medieval field pattern. These were no doubt fields that were farmed when the barrows and later hill fort were built on Old Winchester Hill.

Westwards along Stocks Lane, and opposite a house marked on the map as Harvestgate, take an L-shaped footpath back towards the villages. We walked through fields of green and ripening wheat, allowing us to run our hands gently through the heads of corn, feeling their roughness repeating as they bent forwards and sprang back. (I know the Romans did this because I saw Russell Crowe in *Gladiator* do exactly the same!) The pleasant reveries do not last long. There's a familiar tune from somewhere; the sounds grew louder – a brass band playing *When the Saints go Marching in* – from the direction of the village.

WALK 13

It's infectious – a brass band, a march, some bunting and we are easily swept along!

History had fast-forwarded in a most unsettling way. It was June 2012 and it was Jubilee weekend. When we met the road the noisy procession swallowed us up and carried us along, across the bridge over the disused railway line and into the villages, all bunting, red, white and blue, young and old – even the dogs wore something patriotic. And then it abandoned us as it turned left down a village street; we carried on in unusual silence towards the first of the churches on our route.

The Meon valley is inextricably linked with the evangelising of St Wilfrid in the seventh century. Bede tells us that the men (and presumably women) of Sussex and the Meon valley were ignorant of God and so Wilfrid took it upon himself to spread the faith, no doubt amongst some of the heathens living near Shavards Farm. Perhaps that is why there are so many churches in such proximity in this part of Hampshire. This first church – St Andrew's – was started in 1230 and folk history relates that it was built to rival neighbouring Corhampton church across the Meon (and only a few hundred metres away). Again, that fallible guide local legend suggests that the people of Corhampton and Exton were Saxons and those on the east side of the river were Jutes. Clinching proof is the supposed very late date for the first bridge across the river: 1805. The elaborate but attractive wooden top of the tower of St Andrew's was installed in 1900, partly as a device that would minimise weight.

Across the river is the much older church at Corhampton. It is a simple two-cell structure and from the outside rather austere looking. But it has some interesting tales attached to it – some factual, some less so. The church seems to have been founded in about 1020 and it is conceivable that the yew tree which dominates the churchyard may even be older. There are hints that the church was built on top of a pre-existing mound, perhaps even a Roman temple. According to the church pamphlet, there is a Roman sarcophagus in the churchyard used 'for horticultural purposes'. The original east end of the church had a pleasantly large round window, but the wall collapsed in 1842 due to road-widening. One of the most notable features of the exterior is the sundial, next to the porch, divided into eight 'tides' rather than twelve hours. The highlight of the interior is some twelfth-century wall paintings in the chancel featuring miracles from the life of St Swithun, the ninth-century Bishop of Winchester, one of which involves restoring the broken eggs of an old woman after they had been knocked from her basket.

If you want a break from tales of piety, go back across the Meon to a road called Allens Lane. Somewhere along that lane is a pretty house verge in which you will see the oddest of things – well, new to us anyway – garden plants and flowers planted in old shoes. There was a pair of dainty blue, heeled shoes planted with small cacti and one male-looking old boot set off by some tangerine pansies. Shoes are incredibly personal things and they are one of the few pieces of clothing that adapt so much to the shape of your feet that they become part of you. I know in Roman cremation burials the occasional pair of sandals or boots, now just surviving as a pattern of hobnails, was placed in the grave. Presumably this was to ensure that the dead arrived properly shod to go on their way in the next world. The modern craze for shoe-planters could have started in San Francisco (I believe there is a shoe garden in Alamo Square). There could be deeper meanings, however. There is definitely something about shoes ... best to return to our final place of sanctuary.

The last church is that of St Peter and Paul at Exton, reached along footpaths through fields and lanes to the north, and west of, the Meon. The church is again of two cells with a rather squat timber tower at its west end, capped with a slate-roofed cone. The church dates from the thirteenth century, but was largely rebuilt in 1847. Apparently Exton church is unusual in having a 'weeping chancel'.

As good as new. These dainty blue shoes have found a second use as plant holders on a house verge.

This term stems from the misalignment of the nave and the chancel, and in Exton's case the chancel 'weeps' to the south (most, apparently, 'weep' to the north). Why the tears? Well, the story is that the nave represents Christ's body, and the chancel his head, so the deflected chancel is supposed to represent his head in death, presumably on the cross. It is an interesting theory and testifies to the ingenuity of human beings to see all sorts of hidden and unintended meanings in the prosaic world around them. Another curious feature of the church interior is the carved grave headstone at the chancel end of the nave. It apparently depicts the Angel of Death summoning the scholar from his books. A worn inscription supposedly relates it was erected in memory of Richard Pratt in 1780 and his wife Anne. This particular angel appears to be offering something in what looks like a flask, while the weary scholar, book falling from his lap, strikes a pose of reluctance acceptance.

Emerging back into the sunlight, we walk our final steps along a lane heading north-eastwards, past Manor Farm, with the chalky-cleansed Meon on our right. I imagine we have to thank the river for most of what we have seen – I don't think the hill fort or these ancient villages would be here if there wasn't a Meon. Generations of St Wilfrid's converts must have farmed the fields between hill fort and river then prayed in those early Meon valley churches. Then I look down at my own boots and imagine their afterlife. Pansies or cacti – which would look best? That lack of cheese sandwich is beginning to take its toll and I fear I might begin soon to resemble that death-bed scholar. And we never found out who Maggie was. So be it – it is much better to finish a walk with unresolved questions rather than complete it thinking you have all the answers.

SOFA STATS

Begin the walk at the unofficial car park adjacent to the A32 and north of Exton (SU 617 212). The total length of walk is approximately 9km (6 miles). The elevation range is from 58m to 193m above sea level. Minimum walking time is four hours.

ONE BOOK TO LOOK AT BEFORE YOU GO

Payne, A., Corney, M. & Cunliffe, B. (2006), *The Wessex Hillforts Project*. London: English Heritage. Available at http://www.english-heritage.org.uk/publications/wessex-hill forts-project/.

WALK 14: JULY

SELBORNE – ON THE TRAIL OF GILBERT WHITE, FAMOUS ANTIQUARIAN

IN A NUTSHELL

The Reverend Gilbert White (1720–93), educated at Basingstoke Grammar School and Oriel College, Oxford, while notionally curate of Farringdon in Hampshire, lived and devoted himself to the natural history and antiquities of his native village of Selborne, very largely spending his time in detailed observations of his natural surroundings and gentlemanly correspondence with other contemporary naturalists and antiquarians. Selborne remains a sort of tucked-away place in the north-west corner of the South Downs National Park. But in the centre of the village Gilbert White wrote what was to become one of the most published books in the English language: *The Natural History and Antiquities of Selborne*.

Two things to mention here. The fame of the book completely outshone the author himself. Our edition of the work (Methuen, 1901) opens with the sentence: 'The events of Gilbert White's life are not striking.' True to that statement, Gilbert rarely ventured from Selborne in his later life, was never married and his rather self-effacing manner is demonstrated by the fact that no proper portrait (apart from a couple of sketches) was ever made of him. Secondly, he is revered much more for his skills as a naturalist than an antiquarian. Indeed, there were those who urged him not to include a section on the antiquities of Selborne in the book. Why? We arrived in Selborne one morning, on the hunt for Gilbert White the Antiquarian.

WALK 14

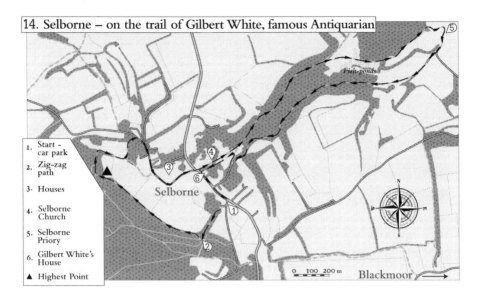

14. Selborne – on the trail of Gilbert White, famous Antiquarian

1. Start – car park
2. Zig-zag path
3. Houses
4. Selborne Church
5. Selborne Priory
6. Gilbert White's House
▲ Highest Point

TIME TO GET GOING

Clouds of different greys shape-shifted slowly overhead as we stopped in the car park (SU 741 335). There is an interpretation board nearby informing you about the different geologies in the locality – chalk to the south-west of the village, greensand under it and to the north-east, clay. Indeed, the High Street divides the geology: chalk on its south-western side, greensand on its north-eastern edge. Adjacent to the interpretation board is quite the most well-appointed public convenience we have yet had the privilege of using in the Park. Just to the east of the car park is a footpath heading southwards towards the bottom of the hill. The hillside is cloaked in woodlands known, in these parts, as 'hangers'. Once at its foot there are well-known paths which I suppose in themselves are now archaeological monuments – the renowned zigzag path to the top of Selborne Common and, to its right, the Bostal, which offers a more gradual ascent. Both were the constructions of Gilbert, intended so that people could walk on the common and observe its wildlife more easily. We ventured up a few zigs and zags, but then opted for the easier stroll up the shady Bostal, surrounded by towering beech trees that made it darker still.

Once at the highest point of the path, from a bench and framed by a clearing in the leaf canopy, we could look down on a little vignette of Selborne, including the rear of Gilbert's house, with its landscaped garden stretching towards us and the village church beyond. He must have paused here too, coming down from the common, immersed in his work and in his world. Continue your walk, now downwards and to the north-east, and once more on level ground the footpath leads you back on yourself and on to Gracious Street, which leads eastwards towards the centre of the village. Along the street there are some interesting buildings. Note a terrace of thatched cottages, now known as Seale View, with a date stone of 1793 – either the construction date or more probably indicating major refurbishments. The stone used was locally quarried greensand or 'malmstone'. Look particularly at the mortar between the rectangular stones. It is an excellent example of the technique of galleting, the insertion of small pieces of flint or ironstone into the mortar to strengthen it. Nearby is the wheelwright's cottage, altered in 1693 as its date stone records. Just before you reach the High Street you will see, on your left, two thatched houses, first Deep Thatch, whitewashed and mullion windowed, then Old Thatch, now largely brick faced. Both these houses are 'baffle-entry' houses, meaning that on crossing the threshold the visitor is faced with bypassing a massive chimney stack, often inserted at a later date. Both houses date from the sixteenth century, with Old Thatch probably the earliest.

Back in the centre of the village, we recall that Gilbert White was a very conscientious recorder of the weather, especially as he was aware that it obviously affected plant and animal life. We have more selfish concerns about today's climate – whether we will get wet, and, more importantly, whether our sandwiches will get sodden. It doesn't come naturally, but we decide to take a risk. Heading quickly across the village green (known as the Plestor – or play place) and continuing at an unholy pace north-eastwards through the church graveyard, we descend the greensand slope to Church Meadow and the Oakhanger stream – a walk that Gilbert often made – towards the site of the medieval Priory of Selborne.

Old Thatch, one of the oldest properties lining Gracious Street, Selborne.

WALK 14

The route here is along a valley bottom, through stretches of woodlands interspersed with meadows known as the Short and Long Lythes, derived from the Saxon *hlithe* – slope. The path is muddy and carried across little tributaries by small bridges. Views are circumscribed by the tree foliage, and even when in the fields the far side of the valley is high and near. It feels pleasantly enclosed, secretive almost. The eye is forced to focus on the close at hand. We agree that it feels nothing like standing on the chalk downs, looking out over the Weald. Soon there are large ponds to our right; some of them at least must be fish ponds that once belonged to the priory. Indeed, there is a surviving priory tile depicting a pike. This reputedly celebrates a minor miracle by St Richard, who visited the priory in 1250. Apparently he enticed a 0.9m-long (3ft) pike from the water simply by blessing it. In a sort of homage to Gilbert, we take pictures of some Canadian geese on one of the ponds. It is doubtful that they existed in Selborne in his time, although they were introduced to Britain in the late 1600s.

A good number of pages, over fifty, in Gilbert White's book are devoted to Selborne Priory. However these mostly relate its historical archive and not its physical remains. The reason is straightforward: by Gilbert's day the priory was not even a ruin – it had been levelled. In his words, the site of the priory was now

Priory Farm stands on the site of the former Selborne Priory. In the field beyond lie slight earthworks, which were probably a priory drain. It's not glamorous, but it's all that's left.

'a rough rugged pasture-field, full of hillocks and pits, choked with nettles and dwarf-elder, and trampled by the feet of the ox and the heifer'. Farm buildings now obscure most of the site. The priory was once a grand Augustinian establishment. Founded by Peter des Roches, Bishop of Winchester, in the thirteenth century, its church and other buildings were laid out around a square cloister. The priory was endowed with various lands and was responsible for the maintenance of law and order amongst the villagers. The priory was also granted a licence to hold a market in Selborne every Tuesday and an annual fair by King Henry III.

However, the very isolation of Selborne may have brought about the premature end of the priory. Far from ecclesiastical oversight, it was alleged that some of the resident canons grew lax in the attendance of services, ignorant of the scriptures and took to wearing fashionable clothes, sleeping naked and seeking the acquaintance of 'suspect and disorderly females'. Selborne Priory was brought to an end by papal decree in the late 1400s at the instance of Bishop Waynflete, Bishop of Winchester and effectively prime minister. The income from the priory's properties and lands was diverted to his new foundation Magdalen College, Oxford. Some have even wondered whether the charges against the priory and its canons were exaggerated at the bishop's behest.

If you continue a little way past Priory Farm, taking the footpath to its north, at about SU 756 346, you can just make out a ditch in the adjacent pasture field to the south – probably some sort of drain from the priory. Excavations of the site were undertaken by two clergymen from 1953 to 1971, the results of which are, at the time of writing, to be published soon. We can only surmise that had the priory survived as a ruin, Gilbert would have done an excellent job in recording the surviving architecture. Although, by way of qualification, we remember that when he went to Stonehenge he seemed to be more interested in the jackdaws.

The sky remains a stubborn grey, disappointing for July, and as we turn around to retrace our path back to the Selborne, rain begins to fall with a steady determination. To be fair, the temperature is not bad, actually quite warm, and we imagine ourselves to be in a stretch or tropical forest as we tramp through the Lythes, listening to the bigger raindrops pattering on to the crowns of the beech trees above us. We can lift up our sagging spirits but we cannot do much to revive our limp sandwiches. Once back in the village we head for a jacket potato in the pub. Gilbert may have eaten them, at least on Guy Fawkes Night when it was customary to bake them in the bonfire. In another homage to Gilbert, we have a melon dessert as we know that he was fascinated with this fruit and used to cultivate it in his garden in Selborne.

Gilbert White's house still stands in the middle of Selborne, opposite the Plestor, but has been considerably altered since his day. It now houses a museum dedicated to him, shared rather incongruously with an exhibition documenting the life of Lawrence Oates, one of the dead heroes of Scott's tragic expedition to the South Pole. The entrance to the museum and the museum shop are in the brick extension, originally the billiard room built around 1900. The earlier house

Gilbert White's home, now a museum. The oldest part of the house is set back from the street, to the left.

adjoins to the south-east. There are several other historic buildings in the village. Just south-east, along the High Street, stands Cobbler Cottage, to which the local vicar retired (he was probably unpopular amongst the locals) in the mid-1600s, having been replaced by a more puritanical incumbent. And further along still lies the timber-framed (now brick in-filled) cottage known as Lassams, probably dating from the late 1400s. Gilbert praised the then owner as an ingenious grafter of roses. But our search for Gilbert is the search for the antiquary, so we head for another of his subjects: the village church dedicated to St Mary. At least it will be dry inside.

Gilbert published a few pages about Selborne church. He was, of course, writing from the context of eighteenth-century knowledge so is to be forgiven for mistaking the age of the structure. He dated it to the time of Henry VII, but the main structure of the church is far older, belonging to the end of the twelfth century. The interior is more appealing than the exterior. Inside the big, round columns supporting pointed arches indicate its Norman ancestry. The church is also a memorial to Selborne's most lauded family. A black slab in the centre of the chancel floor commemorates the grandfather of the naturalist, another Gilbert White, Vicar of Selborne from 1681 to 1728. His grandson, our Gilbert the naturalist and antiquarian, is remembered in a memorial tablet on the south side of the altar. More colourful are some wonderful stained-glass windows in Gilbert's honour. One depicts St Francis preaching to all the birds identified in Gilbert's book. The other carries a central roundel with animals, including a hedgehog and a bat, falling oak and beech leaves and a description of Gilbert as 'a humble student of nature'.

From the outside the church looks rather dour and solid, an impression strengthened by a rather low, square tower at its western end. The effect is not enhanced by the crazy-paving-style stonework applied to the walls by zealous Victorian restoration. At least Gilbert did not have to deal with overbearing Victorian architects. Not far from the entrance porch is the stunted trunk of a yew tree, another one of Gilbert's subjects. A sign at its base indicates that it was designated by the queen in 2002, the year of her Golden Jubilee, as one of the great British trees in our national heritage. Gilbert describes the tree as having a girth of 7m (23ft) and thought it as old as the church and therefore could be deemed an antiquity. He warns the reader that eating just a small amount of berries and twigs of the yew will bring almost certain death to cows and horses, although turkeys, sheep and deer seem unaffected. As to the purpose of the tree, and their frequent presence in churchyards, Gilbert speculates that yews might give protection to the structure of churches (by shielding them from winds) or afford shelter to a congregation or be for the manufacture of longbows or, perhaps, owing to their 'funereal appearance', might be an emblem of immortality. The Romans seem to have associated yews with death and mourning, so Gilbert's last suggestion seems more believable.

But, of course, the visitor today soon appreciates that the yew of Gilbert's day is no more. At ten past three, on the afternoon of Thursday, 25 January 1990,

a fierce gust of wind roared from the west and uprooted the yew, flinging it down with what contemporary accounts describe as 'a mighty crash'. Photographs of the prone tree show that it still retained a circular bench around its base, now at an almost vertical angle, rather like a seat on a suddenly stilled fairground ride. Experts were called in to assess what steps could be taken to remedy the situation. Archaeologists excavated in the hole left by the uprooted yew and

The memorial window to Gilbert White in the church at Selborne. It is perhaps a little more forthcoming than Gilbert might have wanted.

WALK 14

found human bones and coffin nails, the earliest of which dated to around 1200 CE and, tellingly, were placed up against the yew when it must have then been some 0.9m (3ft) in diameter. Tree experts suggested the yew could have been even older, perhaps dating back to the mid-Saxon period and the time of conversions to Christianity. Valiant attempts were made at resurrection, with the hope that the tree, once righted, might put down fresh roots and grow sturdy again. Nature was not to be persuaded, however; no re-growth occurred. Now only sweet honey-suckle adorns the trunk.

Just beyond the churchyard is a millennium seat, where villages and friends welcomed the third millennium to the accompaniment of fireworks, a lighted beacon and pealing bells. In the sodden weather its metal seat looks especially uninviting but we gingerly sit down to make sense of the things we have seen on our walk. Still hungry, we check on the state of our sandwiches – we need food for thought but they remain limply damp. Secondly, we think we can see the quarry in Huckers Lane, a short distance to the east, where stone for the church was obtained; it is conveniently close. Thirdly, and a little more philosophically, we reflect that people advised Gilbert not to include the section on antiquities in his book. They said the public would find it boring. And we know he wasn't always correct. We agree that the sections of his book on the animals, especially birds and plants, are the most remarkable. Nevertheless, he wasn't always right about them either, famously arguing that that swallows and other birds might not migrate to winter sun abroad but lurk hidden in the neighbourhood.

And what connections are there between the book, the man and the village? Gilbert loved Selborne, staying there for much of his later life. He took some delight in its secluded nature, often commenting on the severe winters when snow and ice obstructed the sunken lanes that connected it with the wider world. He himself was no traveller, notoriously suffering from stagecoach sickness. That sense of being cut off, the shortened views in a landscape which hid distant horizons, encouraged a focus on immediate surroundings, on the plant and animal life of the village, its fields, its woods. The minute particulars of the seasonal growth and decay, appearance and disappearance, were there to record in conscientious fashion. The wonder and complexity of it all produced the reticent author. We speculate whether Gilbert's attachment to Selborne actually influenced his views of bird migration. Why would swallows want to leave for the winter when he didn't?

We walk back through the churchyard hoping that the sun might at last break through. It doesn't. In his will Gilbert specifically stated that he wanted to be buried in the churchyard at Selborne in 'as plain and private a way as possible without any pall bearers or parade'. In death, as in life, his sense of reserve was a common thread. We find his grave, just as he would have wanted it, tucked away on the north side of the chancel, away from the entrance to the church, marked only by a simple inscribed stone: 'G. W. 26th June 1793'. But it is in the brilliant observations of *The Natural History and Antiquities of Selborne* that he achieved an unexpected and unsought for immortality.

SOFA STATS

Begin the walk at the car park next to the Selborne Arms (SU 741 335). The total length of walk is approximately 6km (4 miles). The elevation range is from 90m to 147m above sea level. Minimum walking time is two and a half hours.

A FEW BOOKS TO LOOK AT BEFORE YOU GO

Baker, D. (forthcoming), *Excavations at Selborne Priory 1953–1969.* Hampshire: Hampshire Studies Monograph.

Mabey, R. (2006), *Gilbert White: a Biography of the Author of The Natural History of Selborne.* London: Profile Books.

White, G. (1901), *The Natural History and Antiquities of Selborne by Gilbert White.* London: Methuen.

Yates, E. (2009), *Knights, Priests and Peasants: a History of Selborne.* Selborne: Selborne Publishing.

WALK 14

WALK 15: JULY

ST CATHERINE'S HILL, WINCHESTER – THERE BE DRAGONS

IN A NUTSHELL

This walk is at the far western end of the South Downs National Park, climbing St Catherine's Hill to enjoy views over Winchester and the river Itchen filling its water meadows between them. Sights and sounds come thick and fast – disused railways, a canal, a hill fort, a ruined church, plague pits, old mills with noisy weirs, a beautiful almshouse and a prestigious college – all set alongside murmuring waters of the chalky-clean river. And there is a fairy-tale surprise at the end: dragons. The walk provides opportunities to reflect on the relationship between the Roman and medieval city of Winchester and its immediate rural hinterland. It was also our last walk of the fifteen we completed for this book. A certain wistfulness walked with us, slowing our progress. We had come to love these strolls. We weren't really ready to take the last steps.

TIME TO GET GOING

The best place to start is the small car park alongside the river and just to the north of St Catherine's Hill, the eastern end of Tun Bridge, roughly at SU 483 280. Before you climb the hill, take a look at the river, upstream from the bridge. If it's a sunny day the line of trees on the bank are mirrored in the water. Actually, this stretch of water is known more correctly as the Itchen Navigation Canal, authorised by Act of Parliament in 1655, built by 1710 and designed to improve the passage of barges carrying coal, timber and chalk between Winchester and the sea. The river proper flows to the west, closer to the modern city.

15. There be Dragons ... St Catherine's Hill, Winchester

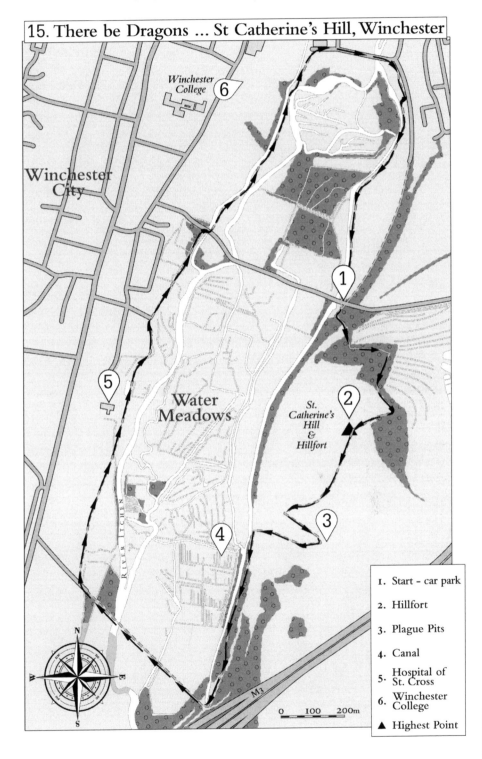

Winchester College **6**

Winchester City

Water Meadows

St. Catherine's Hill & Hillfort

River Itchen

1

2

3

4

5

M3

N
S
E
W

0   100   200m

1. Start – car park
2. Hillfort
3. Plague Pits
4. Canal
5. Hospital of St. Cross
6. Winchester College
▲ Highest Point

WALK 15

South of the car park you come up fast against a brick-built bridge of the now disused railway linking Didcot and Southampton. The line was completed in 1891 and saw important service during the Second World War, ferrying soldiers and equipment to the Channel. It failed to generate sufficient revenue in the post-war period and was an obvious target for closure in the 1960s. Hard by the bridge is an interpretation board, providing you with a synopsis of the hill fort and other monuments on top of the hill. We noted that the text recommended that, in the guise of an Iron Age farmer, you imagined yourself running up the hill for cover as a warning cry rings out over the valley. Some things are best left to the imagination. We walked with a defiant sedateness through the brick railway arch, sun shining at its far end and into another world.

Take the path upwards a little then the flat section along to the east. Soon you come to a right angle, followed by some steps in the hillside that will take you to towards the summit. You should eventually climb over the outer, or counterscarp, bank of the hill fort and descend into its ditch its northern side. The big inner bank, tree covered, is in front of you, to the south. Now linger in this special place. It is heavily shaded and dried leaves and beech mast litter the ground. Just occasionally a strong sun will break through, creating pools of light. Overhead the trees form a curving canopy. If time travel ever became a possibility then surely it would start here, along this tunnel. Walk south-eastwards, along the bottom of the ditch, until you come to a break in the inner bank, to your right: the entrance to the hill fort. Perhaps some Iron Age youths, guarding the entrance, will shout and block

The curving earthwork bank around the south-eastern side of the hill fort on St Catherine's Hill, Winchester. A good place to spot flowers and butterflies.

your path. But we venture in, past the in-turned earthworks flanking the gate, to see only a very determined-looking man jogging with his dog. Neither of them take any notice of us.

Inside the hill fort there is a flattish summit, but the land slopes downwards on all sides to the rampart – formed by a simple 'dump' chalk bank, fronted by a ditch and counterscarp. The main period of activity appears to have been from 400 to 300 BCE, after which the fort seems to have witnessed much less intensive use. The rampart is some way down the slope, especially on the western side, suggesting that whatever happened in the interior was very observable, on display if you like, from the valley below. Certainly from the rampart on the west side there is an enjoyable panorama of Winchester. However, there lies the problem. We know very little about what did go on in the interior. No round-houses or four-poster granaries are known, since previous excavations were small scale and mostly confined to the gateway and ramparts. More recent geophysical surveys have suggested a concentration of ditches and pits near the summit, south of the trees, but only excavation can test their date, function and plan.

The most obvious feature on the hilltop is the clump of beech trees in the centre, so walk towards it. Before you reach the copse you come upon a maze cut into the grass. This is likely to date from the seventeenth century and was presumably used for recreation. It is often attributed to Winchester College, who called it 'Labyrinth', but history suggests that they viewed it with disdain as it interfered with their particular code of football played on this flat grassy space.

The beech copse on St Catherine's Hill. The slight mound is all that is left of the twelfth-century chapel.

WALK 15

A path of some 624m lies within its overall rectangular form. Now stroll on between the trees and as your eyes adjust to the reduced light levels you can make out a low mound. This is the site of a chapel, erected before the middle of the twelfth century, cross shaped in plan with a central tower, and dedicated to St Catherine, apparently the patron saint of hills. It was reduced to rubble during the English Reformation. A bank to the west formed part of the chapel enclosure and perhaps bounded a cemetery. Use your imagination to picture the barefoot devout solemnly walking from Winchester, praying their way to a service in the hilltop chapel. The clump or copse of beech trees is, of course, an artefact in its own right. It was planted by Lord Botetourt in the late 1700s, during the last encampment of the local militia and was apparently completed in one day. Some of the outside trunks still form a neat and planned arc and many carry early inscriptions, now stretched and bark-blurred.

Walk to the south side of the hill fort, and stretching in front of you is a flight of steps, leading you down towards the valley bottom and its complex of water meadows. Once you reach level ground turn to the left a moment, away from the river. You should see a number of depressions in the ground. These are the remains of plague pits, probably seventeenth century in date, where bodies of the infected, carted out from Winchester in the dead of the night, would be unceremoniously dumped and quickly covered with earth. Samuel Pepys and Daniel Defoe wrote graphically of the horrors of the disease as it struck London in 1665. The citizens of Winchester would have avoided St Catherine's Hill 'like the plague' at that time – although we doubt they used that expression. We don't linger long either, and are relieved to join the main path by the river/canal; the water's refreshingly clear and the trailing manes of water crowfoot a dazzling green.

When you come out by the canal there is an interpretation board. It tells the story of a sawmill that stood on the other side of the canal in the nineteenth century. If you lean over the railings you can make out the curved brickwork that housed the waterwheel, providing power for the saws, and the remains of a lock. You are reminded that you are standing on a towpath and a picture of a coal-laden barge brings back sights and sounds now largely lost. Timber must have been loaded on to barges and transported down to Southampton, while other barges were towed upwards by draft horses, carrying coal for the residents of Winchester. In the past the main waterways of the National Park, such as the Ouse, Adur, Arun and Itchen, were busy thoroughfares alive with cargoes carried by barges and small boats, the air full of shouts from barges, lock-keepers and porters. Nowadays we have the M3, roaring past the other side of St Catherine's Hill – not quite so much fun and no chance of any snatched conversation.

Take the towpath southwards, flat and shaded, the canal hidden to your right. To your left is a large bank, very straight-topped. Once it carried trains towards Southampton, big steam engines whistling and hissing their way towards the coast, trailing carriages of people or wagons full of freight. You could hear and smell the engines a long time before you saw them. Now it's silent – another thing to blame the M3 for, perhaps a tad unjustly. Soon, after walking beneath a bridge as the railway line crosses the towpath, you come to a sign pointing right to St Cross. Take this narrow but very straight path across the canal, river and water meadows. There are good views towards St Catherine's Hill and up and down the river on the western side of the meadows, and south towards the viaduct, currently being restored in preparation for a Sustrans cycle path. Turn to the north, walking on paths on the Winchester side of the river. There is a complex of old buildings to the right, which look at one stage as if they included a mill, and there is what appears to be a Second World War pillbox nearby. We don't investigate for two reasons: we are getting hungry and we are unsure about the public accessibility of the footpath that leads up to it.

A little further on, and just a little to your left, is the magnificent medieval complex of the Hospital of St Cross: a twelfth-century church and fifteenth-century almshouse. It is just outside the western boundary of the South Downs National Park, but to ignore it would be foolish, and besides, just by its south side there is a very pleasant bench, facing southwards, invitingly empty and fit for a king and queen's feast. Royalty is nowhere to be seen, so we sit and plunder our rucksack for foil-wrapped sandwiches. Now, that most trustworthy and popular of local guides, a lad called Legend, has it that Henry de Blois, Bishop of Winchester,

was stopped hereabouts one day in the twelfth century by a young peasant girl who begged him to help her starving people. Much moved, indeed much taken, he ordered the construction of the hospital, which is now, allegedly, Britain's oldest charitable institution. The hospital housed thirteen men who were so weak that they were unable to work and fed 100 more at its gates each day. These thirteen eventually became the Brothers of St Cross, not monks, since to this day the hospital is a secular foundation.

The Hospital of St Cross outside the medieval city of Winchester. It looks substantial and solid, befitting its Norman ancestry.

WALK 15

In the fifteenth century, Cardinal Beaufort created the Order of Noble Poverty, adding the splendid almshouse to the existing hospital buildings and giving St Cross the look that it has today. It is a stunning assembly of buildings. The church is late Norman with its squat square tower; there is a later turreted gatehouse, a brotherhood hall with its central hearth and finally a tall-chimneyed almshouse. Just as we finished our lunch, warmed and gently fattening in the sun, we read about the Wayfarer's Dole. Apparently any visitor can come to the Porter's Gate and request a drink of beer and some bread to help it down. We feel we qualify on all counts: we are travellers (sort of); we have journeyed east–west through the South Downs National Park to complete these fifteen walks (a pilgrimage of sorts); and we bear our poverty nobly. Temptation beckons us in the direction of the porter. But just as we step towards our breaded beer, two swans fly overhead, landing ungainly and noisily on the Itchen. Surely a sign, so Legend says, and we earnestly return eastwards to the river path, turning northwards and leaving our Wayfarer's Dole for the more deserving.

The river path is pleasant and varied, part wooded, and again with wide views towards St Catherine's Hill to the east. You can clearly see the interior of the fort from this path, confirming that what went on inside was not secret, but there for people to see and note. Others have enjoyed this route too. There is a welcoming bench dedicated to Max, who enjoyed 'sky-larking'. The plaque invites us to sit and share a story with him. So we do. There are further signs along this stretch of water of old riverside mills, but the most elegant building, glimpsed to the left across the playing field, is the pedimented and brick façade of one of the many historic buildings that make up Winchester College.

The college was founded at the end of the fourteenth century by William of Wykeham, Bishop of Winchester and Chancellor (in reality Prime Minister) of England. At that time, learning and literacy were the province of the Church, and the college's job was to see that the king was supported in a multitude of administrative tasks by a well-educated clergy. The semi-monastic institution survived the Reformation, probably because of its links with New College, Oxford. Gradually, its post-Reformation role focused more on teaching commoners rather than its own in-house scholars. The brick-built school, added to its medieval stone predecessor, developed from the end of the seventeenth century. The baroque-styled façade across the playing fields, with its Ionic columns and slightly projecting centre and wings, is the College Science School, and dates from 1904. To attend Winchester College it helps if you are bright and your parents have deeper pockets than most. The current boarding fees for a year are in excess of £30,000. We feel that St Cross, with its emphasis on noble poverty, is more our sort of place.

Past the college buildings, take a right, along College Walk and across the river and canal once more. You pass some elegant houses, one a lovely stuccoed-taupe colour with white door and Georgian fan light, and then drop down to the side of the canal, heading southwards. It's a good place to look up and down the waterway; reflections of old brick canal-side buildings, now converted, are a reminder

Steady now! Row hard, but don't rock the boat!

of the area's transport history. We amble along, tiring now, in single file since the path is not wide. The sounds of voices and laughter ahead then slowly start to intrude. There is much thrashing on the canal as we approach the grassed space, our final walk's end, just north of St Catherine's Hill. We have stumbled upon the closing stages of the Winchester Dragon Boat Festival, gracing the late afternoon of Sunday, 15 July 2012.

Now we are both new to the phenomenon of dragon boat racing. Where have we been all these years? Teams of rowers compete with each other along this stretch of canal seated in narrow wooden boats, each of which has a prow carved and gaily painted in the shape of a dragon's head. Dragon-boating hails from China and is now a well-organised worldwide sport, often attracting local rowers who raise money for charity. I liked the symbolism – the boat as the dragon's body, the rowers as its limbs, the prow-seated rhythmical drummer as its heartbeat and its head, well, as its head. Every tradition, even an imported one, has to have a first day, and maybe people will write of the antiquity of dragon boats on the Itchen at some distant point in the future. Perhaps. We feel peckish and thirsty again and it's too far to walk back and claim our Wayfarer's Dole. We opt for something a little more secular and head towards the dragon-dressed man in the dragon-burger van. As we approach the man-van-dragon, he is clicking his fingers to the pop song played over the tannoy – *Don't Rock the Boat*. We grin. We do rock a lot. But will we capsize?

WALK 15

SOFA STATS

The starting point for this walk is the small car park to the north of St Catherine's Hill, roughly at SU 483 280. The total length of walk is approximately 6km (4 miles). The elevation range is from 28m to 94m above sea level. Minimum walking time is one and a half hours.

ONE OR TWO BOOKS TO LOOK AT BEFORE YOU GO

Legg, P. (2011), *Winchester: History You Can See*. Stroud: The History Press. (This book concentrates more on Winchester as a historic city, but it does include a chapter on the environs, including St Catherine's Hill, and has an up-to-date bibliography for further reading).

Payne, A., Corney, M. & Cunliffe, B. (2006), *The Wessex Hillforts Project*. London: English Heritage. For detailed information on St Catherine's Hill. Available at http://www.english-heritage.org.uk/publications/wessex-hill forts-project/.

GETTING AROUND THE PARK

VISITING SITES

Anywhere in and around the South Downs National Park

The South Downs National Park is unusual among national parks in having a relatively minor percentage of its area in public ownership. However, there are plenty of actual historic and archaeological sites in public or charitable ownership that you can visit, and the whole Park is well served by footpaths and other trails. A selection of the major visitable sites is indicated on the main map of the Park in this book (see colour section). For a few of the principal archaeological or historic attractions, like Bignor Roman Villa or Petworth House, there is an admission charge to pay. For most, like Old Winchester Hill, Hampshire or Devil's Dyke, near Brighton, access is free. The South Downs Way will also take you close to some of the Park's key monuments. Also, don't forget to visit many of the museums scattered in and around the Park. Many are free to enter and offer additional information on the region's history and archaeology.

Our Walks in the South Downs National Park

The walks featured in this book (located on the geological map of the Park) almost always follow public footpaths and do not include any sites or monuments where there is an entry charge. The only site where we advise you to alert the owners in advance is the flint mines on Harrow Hill (contact details are provided at the end of the text for that walk). Although we start most of our walks in a car park, you can, of course, investigate how to access the starting points by way of public transport. Note that public conveniences, apart from towns and villages, are not frequent. However, in Selborne, even if you don't need them, do take a look at the impressive example in the village car park.

THE COUNTRYSIDE CODE

Remember when you visit the Park to follow the good common sense outlined in the Countryside Code: www.naturalengland.org.uk. You can also find plenty of very useful information, for instance on the types of access and paths available in the countryside, on the Ramblers website: www.ramblers.org.uk/info/britain/access-for-walkers-in-britain.htm. Make sure you wear sensible clothing and footwear, and carry gloves and a hat – suffering from wind chill on the Downs can take the edge off the beauty of the scenery! If you can tell a friend or neighbour where you are going in advance, so much the better. And always carry a compass, a map (the Ordnance Survey Explorer Range at 1:25,000 is excellent), a mobile phone, a small first-aid kit and a whistle. Smart phones include the added advantage of being able to display an aerial photograph of a monument or landscape. GPS instruments are very useful, especially in conjunction with maps, and also have the advantage of working in areas of the Park where there is no mobile phone signal, but don't rely overmuch on your screen-delivered data. After all, past generations enjoyed the Downs through their bodily senses and, if you want to get closer to those forebears, you should too. If you are going to be out for some time carry a rucksack with water, sandwiches and a flask of something hot. Even the ancients ate, so no problem there!

GENERAL REFERENCES

Baker, D. (forthcoming), *Excavations at Selborne Priory 1953–1969*. Hampshire: Hampshire Studies Monograph.

Barber, M., *et al.* (1999), *The Neolithic Flint mines in England*. Swindon: English Heritage.

Borrow, G. (1977 [1862]), *Wild Wales*. London: Fontana.

Brandon, P. & Short, B. (1999), *The South East from AD 1000*. Harlow: Longman.

Brandon, P. (2006), *The South Downs*. Chichester: Phillimore.

Brent, C. (1993), *Georgian Lewes, 1714–1830: The Heyday of a County Town*. Lewes: Colin Brent Books.

Bruneau, W. (2003), 'New Evidence on Life, Learning and Medical Care at Beacon Hill School', *Russell: the Journal of Bertrand Russell Studies*, Vol. 23, Iss. 2, Article 13. Available at http://digitalcommons.mcmaster.ca/russelljournal/vol23/iss2/13.

Davies, H. (2008), *Roman Roads in Britain*. Oxford: Shire Publications.

Drewett, P., Rudling, D. & Gardiner, M. (1988), *The South East to AD 1000*. Harlow: Longman.

Goodfield, J. & Robinson, P. (2007), *Stanmer & the Pelham Family*. Brighton: BN1 Publishing.

Hick, K. (2005), *Petersfield: A History & Celebration*. Salisbury: The Francis Frith Collection.

Ingold, T. (2007), *Lines: a Brief History*. London: Routledge.

Leaton, E., *et al.* (1996), *A Petersfield Perambulation*. Petersfield: Petersfield Area Historical Society.

Legg, P. (2011), *Winchester: History You Can See*. Stroud: The History Press.

Leslie, K. & Short, B. (eds) (1999), *An Historical Atlas of Sussex*. Chichester: Phillimore.

Mabey, R. (2006), *Gilbert White: a Biography of the Author of the Natural History of Selborne*. London: Profile Books.

Macfarlane, R. (2012), *The Old Ways*. London: Hamish Hamilton.

Mangles, J.H. & Knies, E.A. (1984), *Tennyson at Aldworth: the Diary of James Henry Mangles*. Ohio: Ohio University Press.

Manley, J. (2002), *AD 43: The Roman Invasion of Britain*. Stroud: Tempus.

—— (ed.) (2008), *The Archaeology of Fishbourne and Chichester*. Lewes: Sussex Archaeological Society.

—— (2012), *The Archaeology of the South Downs National Park: An Introduction*. Lewes: Sussex Archaeological Society.

McOmish, D. & Topping, P. (2007), 'The Archaeology of the South Downs', in Smart, G. & Brandon, P. (eds), *The Future of the South Downs*. Chichester: Packard Publishing.

Nairn, I. & Pevsner, N. (2003), *The Buildings of England: Sussex*. Yale University Press: New Haven and London.

Oswald, A., *et al.* (2001), *The Creation of Monuments: Neolithic Causewayed Enclosures in the British Isles*. Swindon: English Heritage.

Payne, A., Corney, M. & Cunliffe, B. (2006), *The Wessex Hillforts Project*. London: English Heritage.

Available at http://www.english-heritage.org.uk/publications/wessex-hillforts-project/.

Pennington, J. (2011), *Chanctonbury Ring: the Story of a Sussex Landmark*. Steyning: Downland History Publishing.

Robinson, J.M. (1938), *A South Downs Farm in the 1860s*. London: J.M. Dent & Sons.

Rudling, D. (ed.) (2003), *The Archaeology of Sussex to AD 2000*. King's Lynn: Heritage Marketing.

Russell, J.M. (2000), *Flint Mines in Neolithic Britain*. Stroud: Tempus.

Short, B. (2006), *The South-East*. Swindon: English Heritage.

Somerville, C. (2009), *Somerville's Travels*. Basingstoke: AA Publishing.

Stoodley, N. (ed.) (2002), *A Review of Archaeology in Hampshire 1980–2000*. Hampshire: Hampshire Field Club and Archaeological Society.

Strong, R. (2008), *A Little History of the English Country Church*. London: Vintage Books.

Taylor, R. (2007), *Shoreham's Radar Station: the Story of RAF Truleigh Hill*. Privately published.

Thomas, E. (1909), *The South Country*. London: J.M. Dent & Sons.

———— (1916), *The Icknield Way*. London: Constable.

Wainwright, A. (2003), *A Pictorial Guide to the Lakeland Fells. Book One: The Eastern Fells*. London: Frances Lincoln.

White, G. (1901 [1789]), *The Natural History and Antiquities of Selborne*. London: Methuen.

Woodward, A. (2000), *British Barrows: a Matter of Life and Death*. Stroud: Tempus.

Yates, E. (2009), *Knights, Priests and Peasants: a History of Selborne*. Selborne: Selborne Publishing.

Websites

www.airscapes.co.uk – more of Russ Oliver's dramatic aerial photographs.

www.archaeology.co.uk – the UK's most popular magazine for the latest archaeological news.

www.britarch.co.uk – Council for British Archaeology; a magazine with lots of info on local archaeological societies and plenty more.

www.culture24.org.uk – good site to find out details on local museums around the Park.

www.english-heritage.org.uk – the national site for England's heritage. Contains a very good section on the archaeology of the South Downs National Park.

www.fieldclub.hants.org.uk – the website of the Hampshire Field Club and Archaeological Society.

www.nationaltrust.org.uk – find out lots of info on all the National Trust properties in and around the Park.

www.pastscape.org – website of the National Monuments Record. Provides details of many sites featured in this book.

www.ramblers.org.uk – lots of very useful walking info.

www.southdowns.gov.uk – lots of info on the new South Downs National Park.

www.sussexpast.co.uk – the archaeological society that covers the whole of Sussex. Many finds from famous sites in the Park are in its museum at Barbican House, Lewes.

www.timetalks.co.uk – contact the author of this book to give a talk, or lead a walk, in the South Downs National Park for your group or society.

INDEX OF PRINCIPAL PLACES AND SITES

Abbotstone 34
Alciston 27
Aldworth House 145, 151, 152, 189
Amberley Chalk Pits 23
Arundel 22, 27, 40, 46, 50-52, 61, 102, 153

Barkhale 37, 43, 61
Belle Tout 19, 48
Bevis's Thumb Long Barrow 54
Bignor 10, 22, 32, 33, 37, 53, 58, 123, 187
Bishopstone 25, 27, 33, 46, 86
Bishop's Waltham 40, 55
Black Down 15, 35, 99, 100, 108, 137, 141,
    145ff
Black Patch (settlement) 30
Blackpatch (flint mines) 107, 109, 110
Boxgrove 13, 20, 23, 46, 62, 125
Bramber Castle 100, 101
Brighton 9, 15, 16, 17, 20, 36-38, 41, 42, 47,
    52-54, 59, 62, 63, 65ff, 78, 92, 94, 96, 187,
    189
Burpham 50
Butser Ancient Farm 31, 63

Caburn 42, 44, 48
Chanctonbury Ring 45, 99, 100, 114ff, 139,
    147, 190
Chattri 15, 59
Chawton 34, 35
Chichester 13, 16, 26, 27, 33, 34, 37, 39, 40,
    45, 46, 49-52, 54-58, 61, 63, 121ff, 132,
    153, 189
Chithurst 47, 129ff
Church Hill 20, 109
Cissbury 20, 21, 26, 48, 62, 103, 109

Clayton; and Tunnel 15, 46, 62-63
Combe Hill 37, 43, 61, 88ff
Corhampton 161ff
Cowdray 42, 153

Devil's Dyke 17, 41, 48, 91ff, 103, 187
Devil's Humps 37, 55
Devil's Jumps 55

East Meon 40-42, 46, 161
Eastbourne 9, 27, 33, 37, 40, 52, 54, 86, 87,
    137
Edburton Castle 98ff
Exton 161ff

Goodwood; and Racecourse 22, 41, 56

Halnaker 121ff
Harrow Hill 20, 29, 62, 106ff, 124, 187
Harting Beacon 48, 137ff
Haslemere 15
Hazeley Down 52
Highdown Hill 38
Hinton Ampner 58
Hollingbury 38, 48, 65ff
Hospital of St Cross, Winchester 18, 183

Idsworth 60
Iping 24, 55, 62, 129ff
Itford Hill 30, 38

Jack and Jill Windmills 15
Jevington 27, 58, 83ff

Kithurst Hill 53, 106, 112, 113

Lewes 9, 16, 27, 30, 33, 34, 35, 38, 40, 42-44, 46, 47, 50-52, 58, 62-64, 70, 74ff, 101, 102, 153, 189-190
Long Down 20, 121ff
Long Man of Wilmington 47

Marwell 27
Meonstoke 33, 40, 161ff
Midhurst 20, 40, 47, 49, 51, 64
Milland 49

Offham Hill 43
Old Winchester Hill 16, 42, 48, 62, 161ff, 187
Owlscroft Barn, near Chanctonbury Ring 119-120
Owslebury 52, 54, 55, 56

Petersfield 9, 20, 22, 26, 31, 39, 40, 42, 47, 55, 58, 59, 62, 63, 138, 150, 153ff, 189
Petworth 33, 34, 153, 187
Pevensey Castle 50, 51, 83
Plumpton 26, 30, 34
Privett 35
Pyecombe 95, 97

River Adur 17, 25, 33, 44, 98, 100, 104, 182
River Arun 17, 25, 50, 52, 182
River Cuckmere 17, 33, 52, 53, 57
River Itchen 17, 18, 57, 178ff,
River Meon 17, 161ff

River Ouse 17, 33, 44, 57, 74ff, 182
River Rother 15, 36, 44, 55, 129ff, 137
Rocky Clump 67

Saddlescombe 91ff
Selborne 20, 22, 40, 138, 150, 169ff, 187, 189, 190
South Harting 138, 139
St Botolphs 33, 98, 104
St Catherine's Hill 38, 48, 178ff
Stane Street 61, 121ff,
Stanmer Park and House 53, 65ff, 189
Stedham 14, 129ff
Steyning 33, 40, 46, 47, 62, 98, 120, 190

The Trundle 16, 26, 31, 37, 41, 43, 44, 45
Thundersbarrow 27, 98ff
Torberry 138, 139
Trotton 129ff
Truleigh Hill 53, 98ff, 190

Uppark 34, 143, 156
Upwaltham 46

Vandalia Tower 137, 138, 143

Winchester 9, 18, 30-34, 37-40, 46, 47, 49-54, 57, 58, 62, 102, 137, 153, 167, 173, 178ff, 189
Wiston House 114ff
Wolstonbury 28, 48, 91ff